Mastering Strategy

Mastering Strategy

Workshops for Business Success

Michael R. Braun and Scott F. Latham

 PRAEGER

AN IMPRINT OF ABC-CLIO, LLC
Santa Barbara, California • Denver, Colorado • Oxford, England

Library of Congress Cataloging-in-Publication Data

Braun, Michael.
 Mastering strategy : workshops for business success / Michael R. Braun and Scott F. Latham.
     pages cm
  ISBN 978-1-4408-2953-6 (hardback) — ISBN 978-1-4408-2954-3 (ebook)
 1. Strategic planning. 2. Success in business. I. Latham, Scott. II. Title.
  HD30.28.B7293 2014
  658.4'012—dc23   2013042850

ISBN: 978-1-4408-2953-6
EISBN: 978-1-4408-2954-3

18 17 16 15 14   2 3 4 5

This book is also available on the World Wide Web as an e-book.
Visit www.abc-clio.com for details.

Praeger
An Imprint of ABC-CLIO, LLC

ABC-CLIO, LLC
130 Cremona Drive, P.O. Box 1911
Santa Barbara, California 93116-1911

This book is printed on acid-free paper ∞
Manufactured in the United States of America

To our families, a constant source of support, inspiration,
and love throughout our careers.

Contents

Figures

Acknowledgments

We would like to acknowledge the support of our respective deans, chairs, and colleagues for their encouragement. And a big shout-out to our students, for inspiring us to keep thinking strategically.

We thank Mark Quattrocchi at Mark Vincent (www.markvincent.net) for his work on our illustrations.

Introduction

Welcome! You are reading the how-to guide to becoming a better business strategist. Written in an easy-to-read manner using everyday examples, *Mastering Strategy* relies on the most prevalent frameworks in business today to build a complete toolkit for anyone to start crafting strategy. By favoring industry lingo over academic jargon, *Mastering Strategy* provides the vocabulary you will need when "talking strategy" to promote your ideas and initiatives in the workplace. The book is intended for those looking for a practical introduction to strategy, as well as those seeking to take their strategic thinking skills to the next level. Maybe you are thinking about starting a business and are grappling with the question, "How will I distinguish my business from my competition?" Or maybe you're involved in an existing enterprise that needs a strategic boost to take it to the next level. Whether you're a novice to strategy or an experienced manager, *Mastering Strategy* will make you a better strategic thinker. Period.

Who Should Read This Book?

When we set out to write *Mastering Strategy*, we had a few audiences in mind. We thought of those of you seeking to quickly grasp and employ the most prevalent and popular strategy frameworks used in industry today. Are you a sole proprietor looking to make your business "stand out" from the competition? Are you a time-constrained middle manager trying to participate in the strategy-crafting process? Or maybe you're an inventor or scientist seeking to commercialize an idea. If so, *Mastering Strategy* is for you.

At this point in our careers, we have taught strategy to thousands of MBA candidates and business undergraduates. At the beginning of the semester, we tell our students that within a few months (for you, it will be by the end of this book) they will be able to

1. identify the competitive patterns of any industry,
2. understand any company's competitive position in its industry,
3. formulate a set of strategic solutions for a company,
4. recognize the risk-return trade-offs of those strategic solutions, and
5. set a path for the successful implementation of the strategy.

This book is not intended to teach you fancy business terminology (although you will add catchphrases and buzzwords commonly used by executives to your business vocabulary). There are no mind-bending theories to unknot, no complex formulas to memorize, and no multiple-choice quizzes to take. Instead, this book will stimulate a muscle in your brain that, if sufficiently exercised, can make you an intuitive strategic thinker. In truth, much of what that muscle will tell you is commonsensical, but that will only become obvious to you after using the tools and frameworks covered in these pages. With enough practice, you'll come to see the business world through the strategy lens.

How to Read This Book for Maximum Payback

You will note that the book is organized in workshops rather than chapters. There are three reasons for this. First, workshops make it easier for you to get into the right frame of mind: you will be learning and test-driving tried-and-true strategic concepts and frameworks. The purpose of these workshops is to favor the how over the why of strategic thinking. By buying this book, you have already decided that you want to improve your strategic thinking, so we assume you've already answered the why. Our other guess is that you want to learn how to drive the car, so to speak, and are less interested in the laws of motion, physics, and gravity. Second, workshops, in the literal sense of the word, are a physical place with tools for participants to work on stuff. Similarly, the workshops in this book introduce you to various tools to help you recognize and understand competitive environments and formulate strategic solutions. By the end of the book, these tools will constitute your comprehensive toolkit to start working on any strategic situation. Let us be clear: any situation that involves competitive dynamics can be understood using these toolkits. Third, no one tool in a workshop satisfies all your needs (even a trusty Swiss Army knife can't do it all). That's why using these tools in unison is the most effective approach to boosting your strategic thinking. As we mentioned previously, all the tools in your toolbox build on each other and work together, in an integrative fashion. By starting from an assessment of the external competitive environment and subsequently drilling down into the internal characteristics of your company, you can, with these tools, help create a comprehensive picture of the strategic challenges and opportunities facing the company. So make sure that you stay in sequence, starting with Workshop 1, then proceeding to Workshop 2, and so forth. In this way, you can be sure that the strategic picture crystallizes for you by the end of the book.

To drive home the usefulness of each workshop and get you to see the value of its tools, numerous examples are provided throughout that span industries from electronics contract manufacturing to retailing to aerospace, and even simple lemonade stands. The point is not to familiarize you with these industries, but rather to show you that these tools and frameworks hold up across the entire spectrum of sectors and industries. Each workshop also contains a "Strategy in Action" section, which drives home the usefulness and applicability of the framework with real-world examples. Remember, as long as there are competitive dynamics at play, these tools, if applied properly, will allow you to paint a comprehensive picture of the competitive dynamics and strategic choices available to a company.

One Last Thing . . .

Brace yourself. Some of you may not like what we're going to say next, but it needs to be mentioned before we get started. Ready? Here we go: there are no right or wrong strategies. In other words, there is no one strategy out there waiting for you to uncover or develop. We can hear some of you exclaiming, "But how do I know that I've chosen the correct strategy?" You don't; not when you decide on a strategy to pursue. To what extent your strategic choices actually work only becomes apparent after the fact, or once you begin to implement them. Sure, it would be great to have a crystal ball telling you that whatever strategy you decide to pursue will work, but that just isn't the case. Much of whether a strategy works or doesn't work hinges on its effective execution, making tweaks and adjustments as new information comes to light, remaining flexible to new competitive pressures, and so forth.

To give you some comfort in dealing with this ambiguity, let us offer an example: Internet company America Online's merger with media giant Time Warner in January 2000.[1] Valued at over $350 billion, the AOL-Time Warner union was hailed as the deal to usher in the new millennium. The strategic rationale behind the transaction was simple: AOL, as the Internet pipeline, would supply its users with Time Warner's wide array of content in movies, television shows, books, and music. Let's pause to think of all the great minds working on this strategy: CEOs, CFOs, investment bankers, management consultants, on and on and on. Mind you, all these folks were paid hundreds of millions of dollars for their strategic acumen. Now fast-forward ten years. In December 2009, Time Warner bid adieu to AOL in a spin-off after having suffered record losses. So why did the merger fail? There were lots of reasons. For one, the Internet bubble popped shortly after the merger. Then the terrorist attacks on 9/11 compounded the effects of the economic downturn. The World Wide Web evolved, with new competitors such as Google and Facebook changing how the game is played today. But beyond these external factors, management was never able to realize the pipeline-content synergies. In other words, great strategy . . . faulty execution.

So here's what's important to keep in mind: as a strategist, get used to working in a world of incomplete information. That's just the way it is. You can spend all your time gathering and crunching data, but there are always going to be surprises: key facts you missed, new and unexpected developments, or, heck, even people working against you. Given these ever-present unknowns, your job as a strategist should not be trying to nail down the right strategy, but rather gaining a firm grasp on the potential risks and related returns of the strategy you decide to pursue.

With that, folks, let's get to the good stuff. Suit up, put your helmets on, and follow us into the first workshop.

Strategy, Defined: What We Talk About When We Talk About Strategy

Consider Workshop 1 the warm-up session. You don't start any physical activity without loosening up first, do you? Similarly, we are going to begin with basic strategy definitions and conceptions that can put us in a limber state of mind.

Strategy, Defined

Strategy! What a great word! It comes from the Greek word *strategos*, meaning "general."[1] When spoken, it immediately evokes images of power, intelligence, cunning, and creativity. In today's business world, strategy holds this special position. It connotes high-level decision making, usually reserved for those at the top of the corporate ladder. You can just picture a bunch of gray-hairs sitting around a boardroom at a mahogany desk, scheming to bury their competitors.

But hold on. We have a problem, and it needs to be addressed before we can continue. The word *strategy* has become such a buzzword that it is often thrown about freely and haphazardly, without much attention being given to what it actually means. "Do we have a strategy?" "We need a strategy!" and "Boy, that's a good strategy . . . wish we came up with it!" all focus on something . . . some *thing* that is out there, trying to be determined. But when we talk about strategy, what are we actually talking about? What does it mean to you? How would you define *strategy*?

Without a specific definition, participants attempting to craft strategies often end up running around in circles—or into the ground. They will talk past each other, because one person's idea of strategy—what it entails, its intended purpose, and so forth—will differ from someone else's. Also, as often happens, some issues will fall under the "strategy" domain, whereas others are purely tactical (or the means to achieve the strategy) or operational. So you see, before we can start talking strategy, we need to come to a common definition.

Let's turn to our handy-dandy dictionary, always a good place to start with the basics. *Merriam-Webster* defines *strategy* as:

> 1a (1): the science and art of employing the political, economic, psychological, and military forces of a nation or group of nations to afford the maximum support to adopted policies in peace or war (2): the science and art of military command exercised to meet the enemy in combat under advantageous conditions b: a variety of or instance of the use of strategy.
>
> 2a: a careful plan or method: a clever stratagem b: the art of devising or employing plans or stratagems toward a goal.[2]

Well, so much for brevity.

Let's take a closer look. The first option begins with "the science and art. . . ." Let's stop there. Science *and* art. Well, which one is it? One? The other? Both? Stay with us for a moment.

Yes, strategy is science. Though a relatively young field dating back to the post–World War II era, strategic management, as it is known, is its own social science discipline, with its own theories, methods, institutions, and so forth. There are plenty of strategy scholars out there collecting data, crunching numbers, and publishing their findings in strategy journals. Personally, we're glad "strategy" is a legitimate science, because otherwise our combined eight years getting our doctoral degrees would have been a complete waste of time.

The "scientifically proven" theories and concepts allow us to investigate an industry or company situation, identify information that is relevant to what we are trying to determine, put that information into the appropriate boxes, and start working on a strategic solution. But the science of strategy only gets us so far.

At some point the "art" kicks in, and the strategic thinking process becomes an inspired endeavor. Human imagination takes over to see the world not as it is, but as it can be. Consider Southwest Airlines, for example, at its founding in 1967 in Dallas, Texas. A competitive analysis at the time would have indicated an airline industry that was deemed fully competitive; new entrants going up against powerful incumbents like Pan Am and TWA faced seemingly insurmountable obstacles. Anyone considering getting into the business would have been tagged as certifiably insane. Fast-forward to today: Pan Am and TWA are long gone. United, Delta, Northwest, US Airways, and most others have gone in and out of bankruptcy in the past decade. One of only a small handful of consistently profitable airlines is Southwest, and all because the company's founder, Herb Kelleher, had an inspired thought: the airline's competitors aren't other airlines, they're the bus companies in Texas![3]

Let's complete our definition of strategy by selecting the most relevant words from the dictionary's definition: "enemy . . . plan . . . method . . . goal . . . advantageous. . . ."

Enemy. This goes to the heart of the strategy definition, in that we need to consider "competitors."

Plan and method. When thinking about a strategy, we are dealing with some kind of "design" and its underlying means and processes. But to what purpose? That's where the goal comes in.

Goal. What is the *goal* of a for-profit enterprise? Is it to make good products? Satisfy its customers? Make its employees happy? Where do other stakeholders fit into the equation? Should companies play nice in their communities? Should they play a role in saving the environment? Certainly these are all important considerations, but we can relate all of them to one conceptual measure: profitability. Indeed, profitability captures many of the aforementioned factors in some fashion. For example, if a company makes products that don't sell, profitability goes down. If it sells a product but customers are unsatisfied with it, profitability goes down. Unhappy employees? The good ones leave, and eventually profitability goes down. Even companies that disregard social and environmental concerns sooner or later experience a performance shortfall. Consider Walmart, with its reputation (warranted or not) for killing mom-and-pop stores, underpaying its employees, busting unions, and so forth. As a matter of principle, many customers simply refuse to spend their money with the giant retailer. On a larger scale, five years ago Norway's government discontinued its investments in the giant retailer, claiming serious and systematic abuses of human and labor rights as its reason.[4] So for our purposes, we will relate the effectiveness of a strategy to its resulting profitability.

Advantageous. Finally, we need to consider the *advantage* provided by a strategy. That is, a strategy should lead to profitability that is sustainable into the future. An effective strategy provides a long-term competitive advantage that is both absolute and relative. In an absolute sense, it allows companies to improve on themselves. Just as athletes try to better their own records, your company should attempt to do better than it did last month, last quarter, last year. In that way a strategy allows your company to effectively compete against itself. Of course in a relative way, your company has to outperform its competitors. Otherwise, it stands little chance of long-term survival.

All that said, we can now craft a working definition of strategy:

> Strategy is the art and science of how one company outperforms its competitors and itself, as measured by its profitability.

Sweet, concise, and workable.

The Building Blocks of Strategy

Now that we have a working definition of strategy, let's think conceptually about what it means to have a strategy. In other words, what do you have to consider so you can begin crafting a strategy? Here we rely on the work of Michael Porter, the renowned strategy professor from Harvard University, to provide the building blocks of strategy.[5] The DNA sequencing, if you will, of strategy is represented in figure 1.1.

If you are going to think strategically, you have to make absolutely certain that all the elements of a strategy's genetic code are present and addressed. By failing to keep any one of them in mind, you just do not have a strategy. It's that simple. A closer look shows why.

Operational Effectiveness. Picture an industry with a bunch of competitors. They are all engaged in similar industry-specific procedures and routines. Furthermore, they all have access to widely acknowledged best business practices, like just-in-time (JIT) delivery, Six Sigma, customer relationship management (CRM), and so forth. A company that performs activities *similar* to its rivals', but does them *better*, will be operationally more effective. That is, it will have a leg up over its competition—but not for long. Because these so-called best practices are readily available, rivals adopting them will quickly chip away any kind of advantage. In fact, as more and more competitors imitate each other's practices, they begin to perform the same. This makes the overall industry more efficient, with the result that rising tides lift all ships, as the saying goes. However, operational effectiveness leads to *absolute* performance improvements within the industry; it does not allow for *relative* competitive advantage.

We like to think of the following analogy: when making a strategy sandwich, operational effectiveness is like bread. You need to start out with bread to make a sandwich, but two slices do not constitute a sandwich. That's where the filling comes in . . .

Positioning. The notion of positioning already starts to address the most important element of what constitutes a strategy: you have to *be different*.

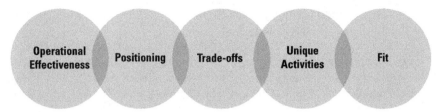

Figure 1.1. The Building Blocks of Strategy

To have a strategy, a company has to "position" itself in another way than—differently from—its rivals. There are three ways to do so: *variety*, *needs*, and *access based*. They're not mutually exclusive, meaning that a company can, and often should, consider all three when trying to distinguish itself from its competition.

Here we describe each one and provide examples. You'll note that we illustrate the positioning categories using a lemonade stand. This is not meant to insult your intelligence. Rather, lemonade stands, to us, are a very basic operation that we can all relate to. We are even willing to bet that many of you reading this book had a lemonade stand when you were kids. For now, to get a firm grasp of these concepts, the lemonade stand example can help drive home the key points. (Trust us, we will complicate things soon enough.)

Variety-based. From the name, you'd think that this type of positioning would entail making and offering a wider variety of products or services. Well, it's a bit of a misnomer. What is meant by variety-based positioning is that a company focuses on producing a subset of an industry's products or services *better* by using a unique set of activities.

Let's try a lemonade stand example: Think of a neighborhood in which Timmy, Jane, and Johnny already compete with various offerings. Timmy offers powdered lemonade at twenty-five cents a glass. Jane also offers powdered lemonade, but sells cookies, candies, and comics as well. And Johnny mixes things up by offering both yellow *and* pink powdered lemonade. For you to distinguish yourself through variety-based positioning, you could offer, for example, freshly squeezed, USDA–organic certified lemonade, based on your grandmother's tried-and-true, old-fashioned recipe. In effect, you are trying to set yourself apart from your rivals by doing one thing and doing it better or in a particular fashion: freshly squeezed, organic lemonade.

Needs-based. In needs-based positioning, a company tries to cater to the specific needs of a group of customers. In this case, the product or service is tailored to satisfy the particular needs of those customers.

In terms of our example, consider lemonade that is sugar free. Clearly, for diabetics, lemonade made with sugar can be hazardous. This would be an extreme case of needs-based positioning. Nevertheless, we may also get customers who are simply trying to watch their weight.

Access-based. Can you reach customers in some unique manner? While access-based positioning is mostly thought of in terms of geographic access, there can also be differences in marketing, distribution, and sales access to customers. For example, Avon uses its distinctive, direct door-to-door sales force to access its customers.

A lemonade stand placed directly at the end of a hiking trailhead could be considered an example of access-based positioning. Rather than wait for customers to come to you, curbside at your house, you go to where you can catch customers, especially thirsty ones.

Trade-offs. Among many managerial qualities, Apple's Steve Jobs was famous for limiting his company's competitive scope: rather than inquire, "What are we going to do?" he would ask, "What are we *not* going to do?"[6] A good strategist will discriminate between the battles to fight and the ones to forego. You can't be everything to everyone, so it is vital to know your strengths and, just as important, your limitations. This means that we probably won't be seeing Hyundai ultra-luxury sports cars anytime soon, if the company's leaders know what's good for it.

Even some venerable competitors have disregarded this basic principle. A few years ago Walmart, searching for additional growth opportunities, introduced high-priced items into its stores, including $300 bottles of wine.[7] This initiative was quickly shelved after sales proved dismal. Why? Walmart's might springs from its huge quantity sales of mostly daily necessities at "everyday low prices." Symbiotically, it can charge those low prices exactly *because* of the volume sales it generates; vendors in fact have to concede to Walmart's pricing strategy if they hope to tap into the high-volume engine. But $300 wine throws a monkey wrench into that strategy. First, Walmart's target customer doesn't buy high-priced wines. Second, Walmart doesn't attract the type of customer who will buy these high-priced wines in large quantities. In the end, the few bottles it does sell afford it neither the negotiating clout nor the logistical efficiencies that set it apart from its competitors.

Unique Activities. If operational effectiveness involves doing similar things *better* than your rivals, then unique activities require a company to either perform those similar activities *differently* or perform an entirely different set of activities that can distinguish it from its rivals. A company's unique activities are the secret sauce on the strategy sandwich, making it difficult for competitors to replicate the exact same flavor. By creating a unique mix of value-creating activities, a company can establish a difference and preserve it into the future. Although this may seem somewhat esoteric at this point, the workshop on core competencies (Workshop 7) will introduce practical tools that can help us identify and build those unique activities.

Fit. Do all of a company's resources, capabilities, and activities work together, in unison, to reinforce each other? Is there a synergistic effect among a company's various activities to "lock out" competitors? This is where the notion of fit comes in. You want to think of strategy in a dynamic way, in which all the inner workings of a company fit together and run smoothly. We saw this in the previous Walmart example: all of its activities are aimed at squeezing costs out of its operation, which allows it to offer everyday products at low prices. The volume sales it achieves in effect loop back to give it the bargaining muscle to receive further price concessions. The $300 bottle of wine simply doesn't fit into Walmart's efficiency strategy.

Let's provide another example to drive home the importance of fit: Neutrogena. You're probably familiar with the company's most distinctive product, the one that started it all (and eventually led to Neutrogena's being acquired by Johnson & Johnson): its "#1 Dermatologist Recommended" amber-colored, transparent, rectangular bar of soap. During the 1970s, under the direction of CEO Lloyd Cotsen, Neutrogena successfully distinguished itself from what at the time seemed an infinite ocean of soap brands.[8] By promoting its pH-balanced soap, Neutrogena was able to carve out a unique and, for a long time, uncontested position among mostly younger women seeking skin care. Figure 1.2, showing the fit among the company's various activities, illustrates how it established its long-term competitive advantage.

Neutrogena's overarching strategy was to make itself the leading brand within a particular subsegment of the soap/beauty products industry, namely skin care for young women. (Can you already recognize variety-based positioning?) To accomplish this, Cotsen and company figured out they couldn't just say, "Here, try our soap—we think you'll like it." They needed to get buy-in from the dermatologist community, which could endorse the product and give it its seal of approval. Neutrogena therefore needed to align all its activities to deliver on the promise of becoming the "#1 Dermatologist Recommended" soap. For one thing, the research and development department had to come up with a product that would actually be endorsed by dermatologists. It then needed to produce a product that could convey a clinical look—hence its straight edge, transparency, and orange tint. With the target market being younger women seeking skin care (needs-based positioning!), the company employed (and still does) young female celebrities in its advertising. In addition, to drive

Figure 1.2. The Strategic Fit of Neutrogena

product exposure, Neutrogena distributed its soap to luxury hotels and spas (access-based positioning!). A favorable experience at the hotel was meant to connect guests to the Neutrogena product and brand and thereby encourage future store purchases. All of these activities were consistent with the overall strategy Cotsen wanted to realize. Moreover, these activities reinforced each other: an effective product received dermatologists' endorsement, which strengthened the marketing message to younger women and spurred adoption by hotels and spas. By achieving a tight fit among its various functions, activities, resources, and capabilities, Neutrogena succeeded in gaining dominance in this lucrative market.

Strategy in Action: Southwest Airlines

We have mentioned Southwest Airlines in passing, mostly because we admire the company's ability to sustain a competitive advantage in a highly competitive arena. Indeed, this company's long-standing success is a testament to its management's maniacal dedication to its strategy. Let's take a closer look at Southwest Airlines' genetic code behind its strategy.

Positioning. Southwest relies on all three categories of positioning to distinguish itself from its competitors. For variety-based positioning, the airline focuses on a subset of the industry's services, in the form of low-priced, no-frills airline service. In addition, rather than use its competitors' hub-and-spoke flight routing system, Southwest employs a unique point-to-point transit approach: a vast majority of passengers fly directly to their destinations, in the process foregoing transfers and connections through large, central airports. In terms of needs-based positioning, the demands of its core customer—the cost-conscious traveler—are simple and straightforward: cheap airfare. Southwest Airlines' access-based positioning has been reinforced only recently. In an effort to keep its fares low, the airline often uses secondary airports, where its fees are much lower; hence, if you're flying to Chicago, you'll have to land at its smaller Midway airport rather than Chicago O'Hare. As airports have become increasingly congested, especially post-9/11 and the related security measures, these smaller secondary airports have drawn more and more travelers looking to avoid the pandemonium of the larger airports. With Southwest the dominant airline in these secondary airports, it has been able to capitalize on this market trend.

Trade-offs. What Southwest Airlines decides *not* to do, strategically, is as important as what it decides to do. Its trade-offs are crystal clear: in an effort to provide its customers with some of the lowest airfares in the industry, the airline has to forego offering any frills that will increase the cost structure of its operations. It has no first-class section, no assigned seating, no movies, and no meals. Indeed, flying Southwest Airlines is a pretty bare-bones experience.

Unique activities. Are there activities similar to those of competitors that Southwest performs differently? Does Southwest carry out different activities? We already noted the airline's point-to-point system; its reliance on secondary airports; and its lack of assigned seating, premium classes, meals, movies, and so forth. In addition, Southwest does not offer any baggage transfer among its flights and other airlines. From a logistical perspective, the Boeing 737 is the only plane in its entire fleet. Finally, since passengers aren't treated to all the amenities available on more expensive airlines, Southwest's flight crew offers a high level of customer service, often infused with good humor and even the occasional rap song.

We need to keep in mind that any industry pioneer invites a slew of imitators sooner or later, thereby quickly turning unique activities into operational effectiveness (i.e., industry best practices). In the case of Southwest, many of the innovations the airline developed, including automated ticketing, have become industry standards. Others, however, remain unique to Southwest: for example, the airline does not sell fares through third-party travel sites. We want to examine how well those unique activities fit together to lock out competitors.

Fit. What makes it possible for Southwest to offer some of the lowest fares and maintain a healthy and stable profit margin? For starters, imagine you're the division manager for Boeing's 737 model. With Southwest as your single largest customer, you will go to great lengths to please that airline. In fact, Southwest probably gets deep volume discounts when it adds planes to its fleet. Furthermore, the airline can train all its pilots, ground crew, and maintenance and repair teams on just that one model. Not only does that lower training costs, but it also ensures that the planes, wherever they may be, get fixed much more quickly. This standardization also helps Southwest adhere to its fifteen-minute turnaround rule: the plane arrives, incoming travelers are quickly ferried off, outgoing travelers are hurried onboard, and presto, the plane's back in the air. Why is this so important? Because in the airline business, you only make money when the plane is in the air and all the seats are occupied. Because the airline refuses to sell tickets through travel sites, it doesn't have to pay any third-party commissions. And the absence of any onboard luxuries squeezes out additional unnecessary costs. Taken together, we quickly recognize that Southwest Airlines is a well-oiled efficiency machine; a penny saved here, a dollar saved there allow this first-rate competitor to keep passing its savings on to customers and deliver on its promise of low fares.

Having looked at Southwest's DNA under a microscope to grasp the sources of its competitive advantage, we should keep a critical eye out for any initiatives that might pose a risk to this efficiency machine. As a case in point, in the fall of 2010 Southwest bought another low-cost carrier, AirTran.[9] Although the acquisition provided Southwest access to new routes, it also saddled the airline with AirTran's fleet of Boeing 717s. Luckily, Southwest's management is strategically in sync, and they quickly sold all the 717s to competitor Delta Air.

Workshop Takeaway

This workshop allowed us to identify what we mean by "strategy." Now we're all on the same page. Also, the conceptual treatment of strategy shows us its basic building blocks and how they work together to make a company competitive. We hope you have already gained a sense of how dynamic strategy can be. Next time you find yourself in a strategy session, make sure you keep asking your colleagues and yourself: Are we speaking the same language? That is, are we in fact talking "strategy," just skirting the topic, or way off the mark? If we are talking strategy, are we being attentive to what it takes to have a strategy? Have we considered all relevant aspects and how they influence each other? Just keeping in mind these questions will put you in the right mind-set for effective strategic thinking.

Understanding the Business Climate: Which Way Is the Wind Blowing?

The first step in crafting strategy is gaining a firm grasp on the overall external environment. You may be familiar with the old adage "Red sky at night, sailor's delight. Red sky at morning, sailor take warning." Well, just like a sailor checking the weather prior to setting sail, you'll be well served to get a sense of the business climate before crafting your strategy. And though you won't be able to control the winds or seas, by continuously monitoring the forces that make up those waters, you can certainly increase your chances of setting the right course and successfully reaching your ultimate destination. In this workshop, we will help you develop the skills needed to gain an awareness of the current business macroclimate; that is, the forces that make up the external environment within which you will craft your strategy, as well as the changes that are bound to influence that strategy going forward. The first framework, P-E-S-T-E-L, presents a series of prompts that can help you gauge the overall business macroclimate. Professor Anita McGahan's Industry Change Model (ICM),[1] on the other hand, provides a more dynamic and already more in-depth view of potential changes that can have a significant impact—positive or negative—in your particular sector or industry and subsequently on your company. As you read through the frameworks and examples in this workshop, we want to emphasize that change is not inherently good or bad; rather, as Greek philosopher Heraclitus so eloquently stated over 2,500 years ago, it is the only constant.

Give Me a P! The P-E-S-T-E-L Framework

What if we were to ask: "What's the present-day forecast for business?" You'd probably feel flummoxed, and rightly so. It's a vague question, the answer to which is complicated, multifaceted, and multidimensional. Nevertheless, its importance cannot be overstated. Monitoring the external environment can seem daunting: in addition to running your business's day-to-day operations, now you have to be aware of your surroundings and constantly on the lookout for any changes. Luckily, strategists can refer to the P-E-S-T-E-L model, a simple yet systematic framework offering a type of checklist of relevant factors unfolding in the marketplace. P-E-S-T-E-L is an acronym for the *political*, *economic*, *social*, *technological*, *environmental*, and *legal* forces that help shape the present and future business climate. By placing relevant information under each heading, you can gain a barometric reading for doing business. At times the barometer may tell you the skies are clear, at other times that a storm's under way. Either way, it's good to know.

No P-E-S-T-E-L analysis can be all encompassing, because there are simply too many factors to consider. That said, we want to give you a sense of its utility by highlighting some of the more critical forces influencing business at the time of our writing this book:

- *Political*: Federal, state, and local government can have a significant impact on your business. For example, some administrations are more pro-business than others. Similarly, Congress can push through or hold back legislation that either helps or hinders industries and their constituent companies. To what extent the politics of a country are stable can also influence businesses. Deadlocks over issues such as the national debt, healthcare reform, gun control, and so forth, can infuse the marketplace with high levels of uncertainty. And of course, tax policy will always be at the forefront of the political agenda. Consider the debate regarding a national Internet sales tax: good news for Main Street USA businesses, but bad news for Amazon and eBay.
- *Economic*: Is the market in an upswing or a down cycle? Gross domestic product (GDP) growth, unemployment numbers, interest rates, inflation, consumer spending, and savings rates all play into the overall confidence of commerce. Banks and other lending institutions will lend to businesses and individuals more freely in good times, turning off the spigot in bad times. Similarly, the stock market provides an indication of the general health of the nation's economy. The financial crisis of 2008 and subsequent "Great Recession" are reminders of the destructive impact economic downturns can have on industries, businesses, and households.
- *Social*: You also need to take into account the nature and composition of the population, as well as larger behavioral trends associated with lifestyles and attitudes. Demographics reflect gender, age, and ethnicity, as well as education, home ownership, and other quantifiable statistics. For example, a frequently cited social trend is the increase in the Latino population and the opportunities available to businesses wanting to cater to this particular segment.[2] Psychographics, on the other hand, take into account the values, behaviors, interests,

and personality traits of the population. What makes today's youth tick? What are the primary concerns of the baby boomers, born between 1946 and 1964? Which segment of the population cares most about the organic food movement, the decline of marriage as an institution, or the next fashion faux pas at the Emmy awards?

- *Technological*: Stem cell research, cloud computing, cyber terrorism, big data, 3D printing: these are just some of the innovations currently changing the face of business. Underlying these technologies are issues of privacy, intellectual property, infrastructure, research and development, rates of adoption by users, and in some cases, the government's approval. As we will stress again later, though we are classifying what fits where in the P-E-S-T-E-L model, all of these factors are inextricably intertwined.
- *Environmental*: Human caused or not, climate change is a concern that affects businesses. In addition to new rules and regulations coming down the pike, disruptions from environmental disasters, including hurricanes, tsunamis, and tornadoes, impact businesses differently. Insurance companies, for example, feel the brunt as claims hit their books. On the other hand, (re)construction services get a lift from these episodes. Finally, issues of environmental sustainability have given rise to an entirely new set of competitors who rely on a "green" sales and marketing approach to sell their products and services: from Endangered Species Chocolate to Method laundry detergents to the Toyota Prius.
- *Legal*: Federal and state laws have different effects on businesses. These laws may be geared toward protecting consumers, regulating industries, or enforcing labor rights. Take the current debate on healthcare reform. Many small business owners fear the increased costs associated with mandatory health insurance coverage for all their employees. This fear may well change their hiring practices in the future. Before crafting any kind of strategy, it is crucial to have a clear understanding of the legal confines of your business and its related industry in general.

Let's consider the direct marketing industry to see how a P-E-S-T-E-L analysis can shed light on external forces that impact an industry and its participants' strategies. Yes, we're talking about the people who stuff your mailbox with coupons, solicitations, and advertisements. Looking at the direct mail industry through a P-E-S-T-E-L analysis, you will see that the business climate over the past two decades has been a veritable perfect storm!

Political: The U.S. Postal Service, the primary channel for direct mail companies, has been in a slow and steady decline, with Congress in charge of deciding its ultimate fate.

Economic: A series of recessions over the past decade has led organizations to cut direct mail budgets or divert them to marketing and advertising media with higher response rates.

Social: Given the medium's intrusiveness ("You're a Winner!"), as well as the sheer volume of direct mailers hitting mailboxes, consumers' negative attitudes toward junk mail have been increasing.

Technological: How often do you check your mailbox? Now, how often do you check your e-mail? The Internet has had a tremendous impact, in that it offers marketers opportunities to quickly create customized promotions and tweak them in real time. Compared to direct mail, online marketing is faster, cheaper, and often more effective.

Environmental: Direct mail carries its share of paper waste. It's often the case that recipients trash promotions without even opening the envelope or turning the pages of a catalog.

Legal: Regulatory changes, including increased postal rates, decreased delivery schedules, as well as a series of new consumer protection and privacy laws, have curtailed the activities of direct marketers.

In addition to highlighting the drivers behind this environmental change, the P-E-S-T-E-L also points to how the industry's formula for value creation has come undone. That is, direct mail companies traditionally viewed their secret to success to be their ability to reach customers. All they needed was a customer's mailing address. In fact, the industry had this down to a science: start by identifying recipients using accurate mailing lists built over years and follow by putting a hook in them using highly effective marketing campaigns. As the P-E-S-T-E-L indicates, the modus operandi of direct marketing companies has been drastically altered.

Industry Change Model

Alright, you've done your initial P-E-S-T-E-L analysis to get a good read on the current business climate. With that under your belt, it's time to shift to an exploration of the *type of change* that may be unfolding in your particular market or industry. Anita McGahan's ICM offers a useful framework to help you understand the undercurrents in the waters you plan to navigate.

However, before we unpack McGahan's model, let's consider how different industries can become transformed by shifting consumer preferences, technological innovations, and other P-E-S-T-E-L factors. To do so, answer this question: Would you rather own a business producing DVDs or one that manufactures athletic shoes? Most, if not all, of you will probably opt for the shoe manufacturer, simply because DVDs are going the way of the dinosaur. Between cloud computing, memory sticks, and other forms of digital memory, DVDs will make nice coasters . . . and that's about it. In fact, many new computer models don't even come with DVD slots and trays anymore. On the other hand, while your manufacturing business will still have its share of challenges going up against Nike, Reebok, Adidas, and others, you can rest assured that consumers will need to purchase footwear for a long time to come (unless we begin to grow hairy, leathered feet like Hobbits).

The previous example may be overly simplistic, but many well-known companies, including Borders, Kodak, and Toys-R-Us, have failed in recent years to anticipate the nature of change. The ICM (figure 2.1) allows for a few additional scenarios to provide some clarity about what may lie ahead in your particular industry.

The model is a basic two-by-two matrix. (Get used to matrices, because there are a number of them in this book!) The labels are "Core Activities" on the top and "Core Assets" on the left-hand side. Core activities comprise an industry's interactions and processes between suppliers and customers that create value in the form of profitability. In the consumer magazine publishing industry, those core activities traditionally consist of creating unique readership content and filling the rest of the pages with advertisements. Core assets, on the other hand, are resources that help generate an industry's profits. These resources are both tangible (e.g., manufacturing plants, retail locations, equipment) and intangible (brand capital, trademarks, technologies, the company's knowledge, day-to-day activities, and capabilities, etc.). Sticking with magazines, core assets include printing presses, writers, editors, and even the magazine's brand name.

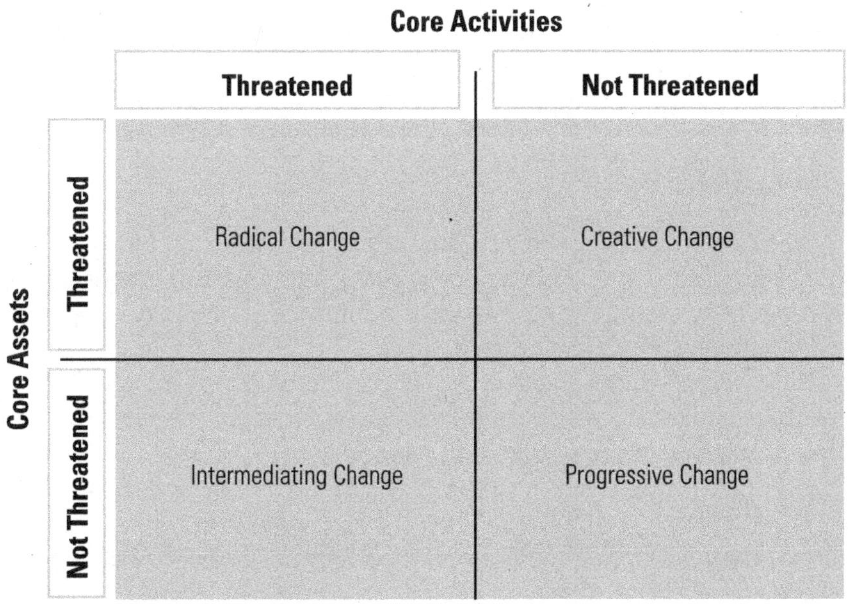

Core Activities

	Threatened	Not Threatened
Threatened (Core Assets)	Radical Change	Creative Change
Not Threatened (Core Assets)	Intermediating Change	Progressive Change

Figure 2.1. The Industry Change Model

Here's where it gets interesting. We talked about P-E-S-T-E-L factors that make up the overall business climate. The extent to which some of those factors either support or undermine an industry's core activities and assets will also dictate the long-term health of that particular industry. As your industry's core activities, core assets, or indeed both, become threatened, they will endanger your business sooner or later. That's why it's crucial for you, as a strategist, to craft strategy that reflects both the nature and pace of change unfolding in your industry. Luckily, the ICM delivers four specific scenarios to help keep you from falling asleep at the wheel. Let's break down these scenarios and provide you with some examples of each.

Progressive Change

When an industry experiences progressive change, its waters are relatively calm. With neither core assets nor core activities jeopardized by external forces, businesses will have clear visibility of where consumer demand is coming from and how to satisfy it. They will compete against each other as usual. Consider the airline industry: core assets include planes, airport hubs, routes, reservation systems, flight crew and staff, and so forth. Core activities include ticketing, baggage handling, boarding, flying, onboard customer service, and so forth. Neither of these sets is being displaced by a P-E-S-T-E-L force. Sure, an increase in the price of fuel will put a strain on an airline's profitability, and an economic downturn will probably cause a drop in air travel. But there is (unfortunately) no *Star Trek*-like teletransporter that will make the airline business obsolete.

Intermediating Change

When an industry experiences intermediating change, its core assets are protected, but its core activities come under fire. And as the core activities become increasingly unstable, relationships with customers, suppliers, and other industry players become fragile.

The fast-food industry offers an excellent example of intermediating change in an industry. In the past fifty years, fast-food companies such as McDonald's, Burger King, and Arby's have snatched up nearly every square foot of prime commercial real estate in America. In the process, this industry as a whole has made sizeable investments and developed significant core assets or resources throughout these locations. However, with American's eating behaviors changing to reflect concerns over obesity, heart disease, choice of ingredients, and convenience, the industry's core activity of offering just its traditional fast-food fare carries significant risks.[3] So what can these players do when faced with such a change? They can leverage core assets to engage in innovative activities (sourcing and making healthy food fare) that create new value. And in fact, we've seen these fast-food companies do just that: consider the McDonald's McWrap; Burger King's Chicken, Apple, and Cranberry Garden Fresh Salad; or Arby's line of whole-grain bread sandwiches.

Creative Change

Do you have an Apple computer, or do you work on a Microsoft operating system? Either way, we wager that you've been exposed to the continuous introduction of upgrades and updates: for Microsoft, Windows XP, Windows Vista, Windows 7, Windows 8, and for Apple, its operating systems with cool names like Snow Leopard, Mountain Lion, and Mavericks. Industries like the software business undergoing creative change maintain their core activities (programming code, testing the operating system for bugs, making programs compatible, etc.), yet their core assets quickly become obsolete. In response, companies in these industries need to continuously renew and redeploy these core assets. Industries similar to the productivity software industry include video game production (EA Sports' Madden NFL 11, 12, 13, etc.); movie production (think of the *Star Wars* and *Star Trek* franchises); and probably the most extreme, fashion ("Try blue! It's the new green!").

Radical Change

When both core activities and core assets become threatened in an industry, it's time to reach for the paddle. Radical change usually arises as a result of massive disruptions when neither the core assets nor the core activities can be aligned to fit the altered external environment. Although many of these disruptions are often technological, others may be caused by rapidly changing economic, regulatory, or even consumer preference shifts (remember the Atkins diet?). Should you face an industry undergoing a radical change, one possible response is to milk that industry to its very end; when the industry dies, so does your business . . . unless you reinvent it! Though more difficult, it's the other, more creative option. Western Union, for example, built its bones in the mid-1800s as the leading telegraph industry, finally shutting down its telegram services in 2006! Luckily, the company had over 150 years to establish its competitive advantage in the money transfer and payment services.[4]

Why do we like McGahan's ICM so much? Its beauty lies in its simplicity. First, it allows you to quickly determine the large-scale transformation unfolding in your industry, either imminently or in the far-off future. In doing so, it also prompts you to think about how value is created in your industry. Second, the framework offers you strategic guidance on where to focus your efforts, whether you're thinking about just starting out in a specific industry or already have an established foothold in it. Let's drive home the importance of the industry change framework with an example you'll probably recognize.

Strategy in Action: Netflix versus Blockbuster

It used to be that there was a Blockbuster in every town. Just a little under a decade ago, the national chain was *the* destination for movie and video game rentals. In fact, for many folks, it was part of their weekend ritual: drive to Blockbuster, beat everyone else to the shelves for the latest movie, go home to watch the movie, and return to the store a day or two later to avoid the late fee. Repeat.

Blockbuster offers one of the most vivid examples in recent business history of how a technological disruption can affect an entire industry (the movie rental business) and, just as important, how organizations often fail to perceive and respond to these disruptions.[5] We'll begin with Blockbuster's response to the advent of the DVD and, more important, its nonresponse to Netflix, a tiny competitor at the time. Once we bring you up to date on Blockbuster's current situation, we can evaluate how Netflix is strategically aligning itself to industry transformations not too dissimilar to those experienced by Blockbuster a few years ago: the shift to video-on-demand.

In the mid-1990s, all was right in the world of Blockbuster. The company had one of the most recognized brand names in America, with over nine thousand retail outlets that were within a ten-minute drive of 70 percent of the U.S. population. Enter the DVD format, the digital alternative to the analog VHS tape. While Blockbuster began carrying DVD movies almost immediately after their introduction, the company's management failed to recognize the nature and speed of its industry's transformation. Why? Because rather than seeing DVDs as a game changer, as well as a stepping-stone to video-on-demand, the folks at Blockbuster viewed the new format merely as thin VHS tapes. For the consumer, however, the DVD altered the playing field in home entertainment on several fronts:

- Compared to VHS tapes, DVDs were much easier to use. Home movie viewers no longer had to hold the fast-forward button for an eternity to get to another part of the movie.
- Because DVDs were digital, they could hold much more data, including additional features such as interviews with directors and actors and scenes that ended up on the cutting room floor. These additional features incentivized consumers to own rather than just rent DVDs.
- A DVD's smaller format shifted consumers' interest toward the prospect of building movie libraries. Five DVD movies could occupy the space of one VHS tape.
- The small format also translated to the retail outlets, where a shelf could hold twice as many DVDs as it could VHS tapes. While this benefited Blockbuster, it also drew the attention of mass-market retailers, who found a new revenue stream selling DVDs to consumers seeking to build their libraries. Indeed, even Walmart got in the game of selling DVDs—and when Walmart enters your market, watch out!
- Compared to VHS tapes, DVDs were lightweight, easy to transport, and more durable.

In the latter half of the 1990s, this last point caught the attention of a serial entrepreneur named Reed Hastings. The frustration of incurring late fees after failing to return a VHS rental of *Apollo 13* on time led Hastings to reconsider how the video rental stores went about their business: Why not create a membership model, similar to that of a gym, allowing customers to view as many videos as they want? To test this model, Hastings mailed himself a DVD using the U.S. Postal Service to see if it would arrive intact. Finding that DVD-by-mail worked, he founded Netflix in 1997. Guess how long it took Blockbuster to respond with its own DVD-by-mail service. Seven years! By then, its looming bankruptcy in 2010 was already written on the wall.

Netflix may have driven the final nail in Blockbuster's proverbial coffin, but it was Blockbuster's failure to anticipate changes in the industry and to respond to those changes that ultimately did it in. At the time DVDs were introduced, the company's management may have thought the industry was merely undergoing progressive change, or at most, intermediating change. That is, in terms of progressive change, the DVD represented an incremental innovation that would preserve all the industry's current competitors as they all moved in the same direction of slowly phasing out the VHS format. Or, if management in fact perceived the change as intermediating, then Blockbuster's core assets, the retail stores, would remain intact, with its core activities needing tweaks in terms of sourcing DVD movies, changing the store layout, retraining staff, and so forth.

Not only did the DVD format introduce radical change in the movie rental business, it also spurred the transition to video-on-demand as video content became digitized. At the turn of the millennium, when asked about the threat of streaming video to Netflix, Hastings replied, "That's why we named the company Netflix and not DVDs by Mail."[6] Indeed, Hastings was no fool, foreseeing the ongoing technological evolution in the external environment and adapting his company's strategy accordingly. Even today, Netflix continues to successfully navigate the crowded waters of streaming entertainment providers such as Amazon, Apple, Google, Hulu, and Crackle (and, yes, Blockbuster, a mere shadow of its former self after Dish Network bought what was left of the erstwhile giant) by creating original programming.

Workshop Takeaway

Before setting out to craft your strategy, it's crucial for you to have a firm grasp on the current business climate as well as any major changes on the horizon. Failing to align your strategy within the context of the external environment can quickly render it worthless. The P-E-S-T-E-L model offers an effective prompt for you to list the most important factors that make up the business climate faced by your company. To gain critical insights into changes that can potentially disturb or even disrupt your business, rely on the ICM to indicate threats to your industry's core assets, core activities, or both. Having checked the weather forecast, you can now pull out your maps and prepare to set your sails for success.

SWOT and Generic Strategies: Starting with a View from the Top

The previous workshop provided us with the tools to orient ourselves in our surroundings using P-E-S-T-E-L and the Industry Change Model. The two tools presented in this workshop—SWOT and generic strategies—are the basis for an introductory overview of your company's competitive landscape. Furthermore, they draw your attention to important industry- and company-specific strategic issues that will require further drilldown, using the remainder of the tools we cover in later workshops.

Square One: The SWOT (or OTSW) Analysis

Many of you will be familiar with the SWOT analysis, originally developed by a management consultant by the name of Albert Humphrey. However, if you feel inclined to skip over this workshop, we urge you to at least read the remainder of this paragraph. SWOT is an acronym that stands for Strengths, Weaknesses, Opportunities, and Threats. Most strategic analyses begin with a SWOT analysis. Unfortunately, they also typically end with it. We have been to numerous strategy sessions at which the SWOT was the one and only strategic tool employed, with participants gathered around a table throwing out whatever they thought was relevant. At the end of the session, everyone patted each other on the back for having engaged in "strategic thinking." That just isn't the case. For one, though a great starting point, a SWOT analysis really provides a static and very limited overview of an industry's competitive landscape. In addition, we have often seen a SWOT misapplied, with Strengths and Weaknesses, which are firm-specific, listed under Opportunities and Threats that generally apply to all industry competitors (and vice versa). This misapplication can limit your vision of new strategic prospects.

Therefore, we want to highlight the following:

Strengths and Weaknesses are internal (specific) to the firm under analysis. Opportunities and Threats are external to the firm and affect all players in the industry.

To clarify, let's build off the Netflix example and understand its SWOT in the present-day movie entertainment industry. This is by no means an exhaustive SWOT analysis, but it should give you a sense of what Netflix CEO Hastings is facing.

Internal to the firm:

Strengths: strong brand, large market share and subscriber base, ease of use, low pricing structure, mail-based DVDs, and VOD (video-on-demand) service
Weaknesses: no physical location, lack of VOD content, distribution time on mail-based service, limited international presence, inability to raise pricing

External to the firm:

Opportunities: increased bandwidth and computing power, VOD adoption rates by consumers, international expansion, first-release partnerships with movie studios, development of proprietary programming
Threats: competitors in VOD (Apple, Hulu, Amazon, etc.), movie rights costs and restrictions by studios, free (illegal) content, postal rates for DVDs

Though Netflix is the only company that deals with the threat of postal rate hikes for its legacy DVD business, this threat could challenge any entrant thinking about starting a mail-based service.

When kicking off a SWOT analysis, we prefer starting with the O and T, or what we like to call the "macros" (although that would spell OTSW, which sounds a bit less catchy, if you can even pronounce it). The macros can give you a quick handle on what the industry is all about: Where's the growth coming from? Are new technologies available? Can competitors differentiate through branding and marketing? Indeed, you can draw from your P-E-S-T-E-L analysis to narrow down your Opportunities and Threats.

Once the list building of the analysis is complete, the next step involves matching up the firm's internal characteristics with the external environment. The two-by-two matrix in figure 3.1 provides direction on how to think through your SWOT analysis in more detail. Doing this brings to the forefront some of the larger strategic issues you will want to work through, using the rest of your tools.

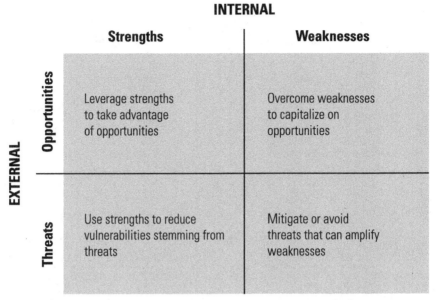

Figure 3.1. SWOT: Strengths, Weaknesses, Opportunities, and Threats

Once you have a solid handle on the strategic elements that make up your SWOT, we suggest you keep them handy for your subsequent analyses. You will need to cross-check to make sure you have touched on all the relevant factors of competition that you initially identified in the SWOT analysis.

Slicing the Market Using Generic Strategies

Michael Porter's conceptualization of generic strategies (GS) is one of the handiest tools in the strategist's tool belt.[1] We just love it. You'll see that its usefulness is in its simplicity—but it is far from simplistic! The generic strategies allow you to segment, or slice, a market by its competitors' product/service and pricing strategies: those occupying the high end of the market versus those using a low-end approach. Where companies fall, in turn, tells you a lot about what these competitors have to do, both strategically and operationally, to achieve a sustainable competitive advantage. Let's take a closer look.

Figure 3.2 is the GS matrix. You will note that it is based on the functions of competitive advantage (low cost versus product uniqueness) and competitive scope (broad versus narrow). Competitive advantage involves the approach to selling a product or service. Competitive scope describes the size and/or composition of the market that is being targeted.

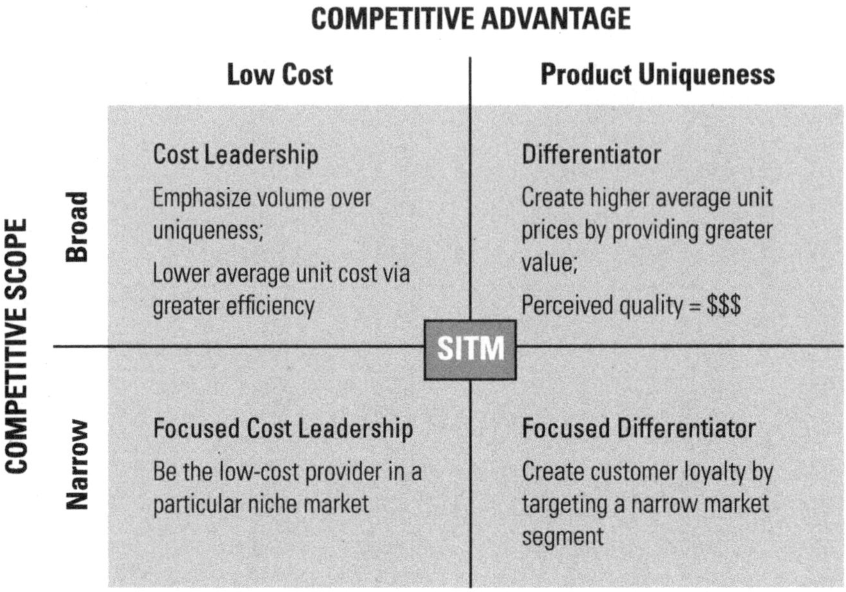

COMPETITIVE ADVANTAGE

	Low Cost	Product Uniqueness
Broad	**Cost Leadership** Emphasize volume over uniqueness; Lower average unit cost via greater efficiency	**Differentiator** Create higher average unit prices by providing greater value; Perceived quality = $$$
Narrow	**Focused Cost Leadership** Be the low-cost provider in a particular niche market	**Focused Differentiator** Create customer loyalty by targeting a narrow market segment

COMPETITIVE SCOPE

SITM

Figure 3.2. The Generic Strategies Matrix

In the most general sense, you can compete in two ways: you can offer something *cheaper* than your competitors, or you can offer something *unique* that your rivals don't. We will start out with companies competing on a broad scope or focus, which leads us to companies occupying either a cost leadership or a differentiator position.

Broad-Scope Strategies

Cost leader. If you intend to compete on price, you will try to occupy a cost leadership position. That is, because your company's products are often (not always) undifferentiated, you are trying to attract customers by undercutting competitors. As such, you have to try to have the lowest prices, because if all competitors offer the same product, the deciding factor in the consumer's eyes becomes the price. To achieve this cost leadership position, it is imperative that you strive for efficiencies that will allow you to offer the product at the lowest price. How do you attain those efficiencies? Volume. "Economies of scale" means "the more you make, the cheaper it becomes." In other words, as your company expands, it achieves efficiencies—and therefore cost reductions—in what it makes. Here, think Walmart, the best example of a clear cost leader. Every week, over 200 million customers visit this giant retailer in the United States and abroad![2] As we discussed previously, when it's not trying to sell $300 bottles of wine, Walmart offers low-priced daily necessities under one roof. Although Walmart doesn't "make" anything per se, it can offer all these products at such low prices because it *buys* them in such huge quantities from its suppliers. It's a volume play! Take Kraft Food, the parent company behind Kool-Aid, Oreos, and Philadelphia Cream Cheese. In 2009, Walmart accounted for 16 percent of Kraft's annual sales—16 percent! Imagine the negotiating clout Walmart has when it comes knocking on Kraft's doors.

Differentiator. In contrast to cost leadership, you may want to occupy a differentiator position by offering something unique not offered by your competitors. Here, because your company is the only one with that particular offering, you can charge a premium in the marketplace. If customers really want the product and can't find it anywhere else, they will have to pay the higher price. This means that your approach involves doing something differently that can create those higher average unit prices. The product's premium may be based on real value, such as a one-of-a-kind medical innovation. Alternatively, it can also be derived from the *perceived* value, or the customer's opinion of the product's value to her or him. Take a $9 Hogwild digital watch: it tells time just as well as, if not better than, a $1,200 Swiss-made Rolex. However, what the Rolex buyer receives in perceived value (brand, status, etc.) is what she is paying for. When considering the wide spectrum of watches available to consumers, from the $9 Hogwild watch to a $60 Timex to a $300 Tag Heuer, the Rolex brand would squarely fit into the category of differentiator.

Narrow or Focused Strategies

Rather than compete on a broad basis, you may decide to target particular niche markets or customer segments, which narrows your competitive scope. These niche markets can be geographic, demographic, psychographic, and so forth, but what you want to keep in mind is that a focused approach pits you against more general- or broader-scope competitors. Companies competing in niche markets compete using either a focused cost leader strategy or a focused differentiation strategy.

Focused cost leader. When carving out a smaller segment based on undercutting competitors, your GS will entail a focused cost leader position. As an example, take Costco, the membership-based warehouse retailer. Costco competes in a very different way from Walmart. First, you have to purchase an annual membership to be able to shop there. Second, it sells goods predominantly in bulk: vats of mayonnaise, cases of beer, and party packs of, well, any popular snack. As a focused cost leader, Costco targets small business owners and shoppers seeking to buy in bulk. In that way, it is more strategically focused on a subsegment of the retail market.

Focused differentiator. As a focused differentiator, you aim to carve out a niche by offering higher-value products or services to specific consumer segments. Sticking with the grocery sector, the organic food retailer Whole Foods fits this profile. Offering a wide assortment of organic foods only— and this in markets limited to urban and suburban areas—Whole Foods caters to a certain type of customer willing to pay a premium for, say, Andean llama cheese at $12 an ounce, if you're into that kind of thing.

SITM: "Stuck in the Middle!"

What happens if you try to occupy a position as both a differentiator and a cost leader? This is where you can wind up "stuck in the middle" (SITM). A company that is SITM is trying to be all things to all customers. Think about it: if you are trying to do something "unique" or different while also focusing on being a cost leader, you may run into one of two problems. On the one hand, because you are cutting corners to save money, you may end up producing a product that isn't up to customers' expectations. Alternatively, the product you do produce may not be price-competitive because its "uniqueness" drives up its costs. In the former situation, your company gets beat out by a differentiator. In the latter, a more efficient cost leader is able to undercut your prices, in the process drawing away your customers.

Some academics have challenged Porter's view that pursuing both differentiation and cost leadership is dangerous. They argue that companies can straddle competitive positions based on both quality and quantity. The example often invoked to make the case for a straddling strategy is Toyota, because this automotive manufacturer has had great success selling good cars at competitive prices. But go back to 2009, and you'll find that Toyota's management tripped up by not paying heed to the potential dangers of SITM. In a race to become the biggest car company in the world (read: "cranking them out"), its quality dropped, causing a series of product defects that resulted in a recall of more than nine million vehicles.[3]

The Toyota example brings up an essential point: it is less important for your company to occupy a definitive GS when the industry is just starting out (few or nondominating competitors, undefined product standards, etc.). In these situations, you have a larger margin of error to experiment with different ways of competing. However, once competition heats up, and rivals pursue their generic strategies, then it becomes essential to stake out a position as either a (focused) differentiator or a (focused) cost leader to avoid getting stuck in the middle.

There's one more thing you want to keep in mind. When trying to identify a company's GS, it's crucial for you to define the market space under analysis. That is, you have to put a *boundary* around the marketplace: the U.S. airline market, the Indian automotive market, mass-market grocery retailing, commercial printers only, and so forth. By doing so, you identify the appropriate competitors that occupy the various generic strategies. So, for example, when considering Ford's presence in the United States versus India, you would encounter a completely different set of competitors and competitive dynamics.

Strategy in Action: Match the Generic Strategy

To get comfortable with conceptualizing competition in terms of generic strategies, let's cut our teeth on the examples below. Take a few minutes to think about each consumer brand and try to identify whether it occupies a generic strategy of differentiator, focused differentiator, cost leader, or focused cost leader.

Mercedes-Benz	Ferrari	Starbucks	Apple
Dell	Southwest Airlines	Kraft	Chrysler

Okay . . . time's up! Let's see where you came out.

Mercedes-Benz. Did you know that Mercedes has a product for every class of vehicle? It makes small two-seaters, hatchbacks, station wagons, sedans, sports cars, sport-utility vehicles, minivans, buses—even eighteen-wheel freightliners! In effect, Mercedes covers the entire automotive spectrum with its product offering—*but* always at a premium. Indeed, customers pay for the reputation of quality German engineering. If customers want to forego this premium, they can always find a cheaper brand alternative for pretty much every class of vehicle: a Hyundai hatchback, a Toyota sedan, a Honda SUV, a Mazda sports car, or a Ford truck. So, given the broad competitive scope and the *premium* pricing, we can place Mercedes-Benz squarely in a differentiator position.

Ferrari. When we consider Ferrari's product offerings, especially in relation to, say, Mercedes-Benz, we can quickly zero in on its generic strategy. Ferrari's automotive offerings are narrowly concentrated on ultra-luxury sports cars, with "narrowly concentrated" and "ultra-luxury sports cars" representing key indicators that Ferrari falls into the focused differentiator position. You won't find Ferrari minivans, trucks, or buses on any roads anytime soon.

Starbucks. Also known as "four bucks." Did you know that if you buy a Starbucks latte every day of the year, you are spending over $1,500? That's a nice chunk of change! Not only is Starbucks *the* differentiator in the coffee business, but the company literally created the premium coffee category in the United States. Though you can find more expensive, specialized coffee offerings, Starbucks, touting more than fifty thousand combinations of coffee drinks at its stores, is the largest premium coffee retailer.

Apple. Identifying Apple's generic strategy is a bit trickier when we consider its extensive array of products. In addition to personal computers and related software, Apple offers iPods, iPads, and iPhones, as well as online services such as iTunes. Consider the fact that Apple held just over 5 percent market share in the PC business in 2012.[4] Consider also that its products are often geared toward more creative uses, such as desktop publishing, advertising, design, and so forth. For the PC business, we might be able to argue that Apple occupies a focused differentiator position. On the other hand, iPods, iPhones, and iPads have a broader scope, although they still sell at a premium compared to, say, Sony MP3 players or Toshiba tablets. For this class of consumer products, therefore, Apple may lean more toward a differentiator position.

Dell. Dell's is an interesting "generic strategy" position that is still unfolding. Michael Dell, while a freshmen at the University of Texas at Austin, pioneered the direct-to-customers, built-to-order model for personal computers.[5] That is, rather than build a computer and sell it through retail channels, Dell decided to take the order first, then assemble the computer to customer specifications, then send it directly to the customer. Not only did this demand-driven model radically lower inventory costs, but it also cut out the indirect retail channel. In this way, Dell products were priced very affordably across the entire range of personal computers. Indeed, Dell was a cost leader. But this position is far from secure these days. For one thing, other PC manufacturers quickly imitated the direct-to-customers, built-to-order model, because there was nothing proprietary about it. In addition, when Hewlett Packard bought Compaq in 2001, it acquired one of the largest PC vendors in the world, which afforded it certain purchasing and manufacturing advantages.[6] Finally, Asian brands such as Acer, Asus, and Samsung started chipping away at the lower end of the pricing spectrum. So where does this leave Dell today? The company's position as a cost leader is definitely compromised, because it is neither the largest nor the cheapest PC manufacturer. In addition, with PC prices continuing to drop, consumers relying on all-in-one devices like smartphones and tablets, and software applications migrating to the cloud, Dell is trying to play catch-up with relevant products and services. Last, a few years ago, the company announced that it would sell its PCs through retailers like Walmart. It's safe to say that Dell is in search of a generic strategy to place the company on solid ground in the future. For now, it remains stuck in the middle.

Southwest Airlines. Let's make sure we define the market space: the U.S. airline market. Though Southwest just announced flights to Mexico, its business is predominantly in the United States. Southwest maintains, "We offer a reliable product and continue to differentiate ourselves from other low-fare carriers by providing exemplary Customer Service." Certainly flying Southwest is a no-frills experience, and as already mentioned, you often have to fly into secondary airports. If you want more trimmings to your travel experience, you can pay up with Delta, American, United, or a handful of other airlines. But you can bet that if you chose Southwest Airlines, you paid one of the lowest fares pretty much every time. Taking into account its extensive nationwide routes and how it caters to price-conscious customers, Southwest can be considered the cost leader in the U.S. airline market.

Kraft. Let's revisit Kraft, the food and beverage giant we discussed before. Let's also pick one product line for our purposes, in this case, Kraft Singles. Differentiator or cost leader? Well, it depends (argh!). If we consider private store brands of cheese, then Kraft Singles could be considered a differentiator. You certainly pay a premium for not only the peace-of-mind brand but also that full glass of milk in every slice! But let's compare Kraft Singles to the Andean llama cheese that sells for $12 an ounce; in that case, Kraft is a cost leader. Now, the issue is that you probably won't find Kraft Singles in the aisles of Whole Foods, so that's why it's crucial to put a boundary around the market under analysis.

Chrysler. Let's think back to the Mercedes-Benz example. As a differentiator, Mercedes-Benz offers a premium product for every automotive class. So does Chrysler: Chrysler sedans and minivans, the Jeep line of SUVs, Dodge trucks, and Ram commercial vehicles. But do they sell for a premium? No. If anything, these brands occupy the lower end of the pricing spectrum. If you were to win the lottery tomorrow, you certainly wouldn't run out to treat yourself to a Chrysler, would you? Well, maybe the Dodge Viper, but that's about it. Like Dell, Chrysler has been experiencing an identity crisis for the past thirty years. Although its cars are somewhat affordable, lower-priced and better-quality products—mostly from Asia—have been eating away at its market share. But there's more: in 1998, Daimler-Benz, the parent company of Mercedes-Benz, merged with Chrysler to create DaimlerChrysler. The thinking behind the merger of equals was to get significant "synergies" between the two entities by using common automotive platforms, consolidating purchasing, leveraging sales channels, and so forth.[7] Well, these so-called synergies never happened, and the marriage between Daimler and Chrysler ended in divorce nine years later. What were the two respective generic strategies? Daimler = differentiator, Chrysler = cost leader. And what happens when you try to do both? Yep, you got it. On the day of the merger announcement, when DaimlerChrysler management was celebrating along with their investment bankers, we both recall feeling a strong urge to reach for the phone and dial the CEO's office to say these four words: *stuck in the middle.*

Workshop Takeaway

We started you out with a SWOT analysis, which will help you identify the threats and opportunities present in the external environment and recognize the firm's internal strengths and weaknesses. Using the analysis, you can get an initial handle on where you need to focus your efforts in order to align your company to its external analysis. But as we said, the SWOT is only the initial step to a much more extensive, in-depth investigation. If you find yourself in a strategy session that begins and ends with a SWOT, your red flags should be flying. It'll be up to you to keep pushing the conversation forward. You can encourage additional strategic thinking using the GS framework: Which of our competitors occupy differentiation, focused differentiation, cost leadership, and focused cost leadership positions? Where is the industry migration to? Who might be stuck in the middle? And last, which generic strategy should we pursue, and is it indeed the right one?

The Five Forces: Pressure Points on Your Company's Profitability

At this juncture of your strategic analysis, you've done a P-E-S-T-E-L analysis, explored the changes in your industry, and conducted a SWOT analysis to get a general idea of your industry's prospects and pitfalls, as well as your company's condition within that industry. Also, you have laid out the various competitors' generic strategies to understand which are differentiators, cost leaders, focused differentiators, and focused cost leaders, and which suffer from being stuck in the middle. The next step is to get a firm handle on the industry's profit potential. You need to ask yourself a series of important questions. First, how attractive is your industry in terms of its profitability? Can you actually make money within the industry and, if so, how? What are the various competitive forces that "chip away" at the profitability of the industry as a whole, as well as that of your company? And most important, how can you position your company favorably to protect against some of those competitive forces? Here's where Michael Porter's Five Forces framework comes into play.[1]

The Five Forces framework is one of the most popular yet misapplied strategic tools used in business practice. What most people fail to keep in mind is that using the Five Forces effectively involves a *two-step process*. The first step allows you to understand the industry's profit patterns, while the second step shows you how to favorably position your company to take advantage of those profit patterns. Too often we have witnessed folks simply filling out the various boxes corresponding to the competitive forces and calling it quits at that. To grasp the real power and value of this framework, you need to first spend time taking a deeper look at its various movable parts and how they work together, in a dynamic fashion, to give you a clear picture of how to position your company as best as possible. Our example at the end of this workshop provides a comprehensive view of how to put the Five Forces framework into action using the two-step process. Let's begin with an introduction to what Porter's Five Forces model entails.

Seeing Beyond Your Immediate Rivals

Who are my competitors? In asking this question, most of you probably point to your most direct competitors. If you're Coke, it's Pepsi; for Boeing, it's Airbus; for Google, it's Facebook. To be sure, so-called rivals are the primary and, in many cases most immediate, competitive threat to a company. But your profits are not only dependent on competitors. There are other "forces" that can undermine your company's earnings potential and continued viability. To get an intuitive sense of these forces, just consider this example: How is the business of Boeing fundamentally different from that of Facebook? If you take a moment to think about it, you can quickly identify a handful of key differences. Boeing manufactures commercial airplanes and other aviation products. As such, it is dependent on thousands of suppliers, who in many cases are designed into a plane platform (i.e., 777, 747, 757, etc.). And its paying customers are primarily commercial airlines and the military. If you wanted to start a new aerospace company to compete against Boeing, you would need a lot of money, a lot of supplies, and a lot of approval from governing bodies such as the FAA, to get even your first plane off the assembly line—and off the tarmac!

Now let's think about Facebook. As opposed to Boeing, Facebook is a service company. Mark Zuckerberg started the social networking site in a dorm room at Harvard. Although growing Facebook toward the billionth user has required continuous funding, Zuckerberg's initial money to launch the site was virtually nothing. Its critical suppliers come mostly in the form of its in-house programmers. Although its users don't pay for the service, Facebook generates revenues through advertising and other services aimed at its users.

Given this brief comparison, consider the following questions: Which industry is easier to get into, aerospace or social networking? Is Boeing or Facebook more dependent on its supplier base? Which company has more demanding customers? For example, how do buyers respond to price increases? Which service or product represents more of a necessity, social networking or airplanes? And which business, as well as respective industry, has more staying power?

This is where the Five Forces tool comes in. Its value lies in allowing you to answer these questions head-on by forcing you to shift your attention away from just direct competitors, or *rivalry*, toward the other four

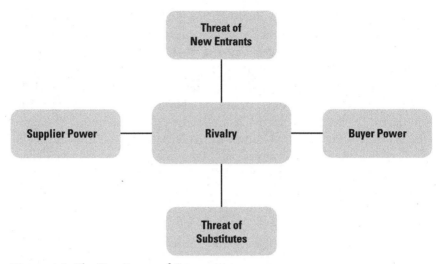

Figure 4.1. The Five Forces of Competition

competitive forces: *threat of new entrants, supplier power, buyer power,* and *threat of substitutes.*

Figure 4.1 is a visual representation of the Five Forces. Get very used to it. In fact, do yourself a favor and burn it into your mind's eye. Looking at any industry through this Five Forces lens will not only speed up your ability to identify the competitive forces, but it will also allow you to clearly understand how the forces depend on each other.

Here's what we want to bear in mind: each and every industry has certain structures and exhibits certain characteristics based on these Five Forces that give rise to different ways of competing. It is these forces, collectively, that decide the level of profitability, as well as the sustainability of those profits. Because these forces can erode profitability, you need to remember that the *weaker* these forces are collectively, the *better* the opportunity for superior profitability. In turn, stronger forces effectively squeeze the profitability out of the industry.

Let's take a closer look at each of the five forces and the specific factors that make them weak or strong. Once you understand these factors, as a strategist, you can begin to think about positioning your firm favorably so that you can lessen the pressure on your profits.

Threat of New Entrants

We haven't even started yet, and already we need to stop and clarify something. Although for the purpose of the Five Forces framework, this force is called "threat of new entrants," in industry lingo, it is most often referred to as "barriers to entry." Indeed, you'll find the phrase "barrier to entry" used even in investment banking pitch books, business plans, and strategic plans. Here's why we bring this up: whereas the two terms connote the same thing, they are actually the opposite of each other. If the threat of new entrants is high, indicating that it is relatively easy for new competitors to enter the industry, the barrier (or the "wall" that a new competitor has to scramble over) is quite low. Alternatively, if it takes quite a bit of effort (funding, R&D, approval, etc.) for a new player to get established, thus signifying a low threat of new entrants, the barrier to entry is in fact high. We will refer to this force as threat of new entrants so that it aligns with the rest of the forces. But just keep in mind that the accepted business jargon for it is barrier to entry. Moreover, if you apply it to the Five Forces framework that is already imprinted in your brain, you'll have to flip the sign, so to speak, when you determine whether the force is strong or weak.

Following is a discussion of the most common factors that determine the threat of new entrants. For simplicity's sake, we take the viewpoint of a new entrant, or a company considering entering a particular industry. Of course, if your company is an established player in an industry, your task as strategist is to consider how best to keep new entrants at bay.

Economies of scale. You'll recall we talked about Walmart's cost leadership arising from "economies of scale." That is, because Walmart makes huge purchases from its vendors, it receives enormous price concessions. This phenomenon also applies to manufacturers: the more they make, the cheaper it becomes to make the product. More technically speaking, a firm benefiting from economies of scale experiences a decrease in the per-unit cost of production as a result of producing large numbers of a good. As a result, incumbent companies (already established competitors in an industry) with economies of scale lower the threat of new entrants. That is, if you wanted to come in and compete against competitors with significant economies of scale, you would find yourself at a significant disadvantage, because you would be unable to produce a product as cheaply as the established competitors can.

Economies of scope. Whereas economies of scale concern the supply side of the equation, economies of scope involve demand-side economies, or when it's cheaper to store, sell, distribute, and market a wider range of products rather than just a handful. This means that you'll be at a cost disadvantage entering an industry with just two products when your competitors are already selling, marketing, and distributing, say, twelve products.

Product differentiation. Maybe you've thought about getting into the soda business with a concept for a new cola. Well, good luck! There are already a number of companies in that business, with a wide array of cola products. Take Coca-Cola. In addition to regular Coca-Cola, it has Diet Coke, Coca-Cola Zero, Caffeine-Free Coca-Cola, Caffeine-Free Diet Coke, Coca-Cola Cherry, Diet Coke Lime, and Coca-Cola Vanilla. And that's just one company! Then there's Pepsi, with an equal number of cola products. And let's not forget RC Cola, Hansen's Original Cola, Reed's China Cola, and so forth. For you to be successful as a new competitor, you would not only have to come up with a different product, but you would also have to dislodge existing customers and the brands they identify with. That would be pretty tough. Maybe you won't get into the cola business after all.

Capital requirements. Maybe you've considered getting into the pharmaceutical industry. Sure, that can be lucrative, but it takes *a lot* of money just to launch. First, you have to make large up-front investments for R&D (all those lab coats and beakers), testing, production, etc. By the time you can actually distribute your product through pharmacies, you will have spent tens if not hundreds of millions of dollars. In contrast, if you wanted to start an online newsletter that reviews and comparison shops cold remedies at local pharmacies, well, you could have that up and running by the end of the day: buy the Web site, put together some content, and hit "publish." The point is that some industries have sizeable capital requirements that deter new players from entering, whereas others have relatively low costs that make it easier for competitors to emerge.

Cost advantages independent of size. As a company eyeing entry into an industry, you may be faced with a hurdle due to incumbents' advantages independent of size (like economies of scale and scope, for instance). Because these incumbents entered the industry before you, they are already more experienced with how to succeed in that industry. Also, they may occupy favorable locations, lock up access to the best raw materials, receive government subsidies, and enjoy a series of other benefits not available to new entrants. In addition, they may have patents protecting proprietary technology or own trademarks and service marks. Like the early bird that catches the worm, many of these benefits accrue to competitors who get established early in an industry, or so-called first movers.

Access to distribution channels. How about putting your efforts toward starting a cereal company? How hard can that be, right? Take some grain, form it into fun shapes, throw some sugar in it . . . voilà. But think about the last time you walked through the cereal aisle at your local grocery store. That aisle goes on forever! There's corn cereal, oat cereal, sorghum cereal, hot cereal, cold cereal, sweet cereal, . . . cereal that lowers your cholesterol, cereal that boosts your fiber, vitamin cereal, kosher cereal, cereal for diabetics, and cereal for gluten intolerance—and these aren't all. Here, not only do you have to overcome product differentiation, as mentioned previously, but you will also have to displace existing cereal makers. In other words, you'll need to convince the distributor to kick competitors off the truck and the retailer to bump them off the shelf. To successfully do this takes a lot of convincing using promotions, discounts, etc.

Government policies. Wouldn't it be great to have a company that makes facial creams with claims that it reduces wrinkles and promotes extra skin shine? These creams can run into the hundreds of dollars, with one brand, La Mer, commanding over $2,000 for a little jar! What a racket! To get started, all you'd need is some goopety-goop and sloppety-slop, mix it all in a bathtub, and pour it into an eye-catching container, right? Well, not so fast. You can't just go around claiming your products will do certain things without the right type of approval. For facial creams, there are plenty of controls and licensing requirements imposed by the Food and Drug Administration (FDA) that have to be met when operating in the beauty products segment. Although some industries have little or no regulatory requirements, others have many. Just imagine wanting to start a business that makes screws for military planes. After first getting all the licensing approved from the Federal Aviation Administration, you would then need to go through additional certification with the Department of Defense!

Competitor reaction. The last factor you need to consider when entering an industry is how strongly competitors will react to a new entrant. In other words, in your attempts to take a new position in an established industry, will incumbent players retaliate, and if so, to what extent? They might lure customers away using price cuts. Or they may steal key employees by making hard-to-refuse employment offers.

Supplier Power

Suppliers can be a competitive threat? Aren't your suppliers supposed to be your partners, who make sure you have what you need to bring your product or service to market? Sometimes, yes. But that's only half the story. The other half is that suppliers have their own agenda, and if for some reason you don't satisfy that agenda, they can start to work against you. Put differently, suppliers can put the squeeze on you by raising prices of their supplies, reducing the quality, or effectively cutting you off. As a strategist, you need to keep in mind not only your supplier's potential stranglehold over you, but also possible ways to loosen that stranglehold, should it take hold. You ask: How can I recognize suppliers who may exert power over me? Well, suppliers are powerful if:

There are more buyers than suppliers. This is simply the law of supply and demand, which dictates that if there are more buyers than suppliers of a good or service, then suppliers can raise prices, play buyers off each other, etc. Here, picture a mother with a freshly baked pie and the chores she can get her kids to do.

Products/services are unique. Which company is the most powerful player in the personal computer business? Hint: Who was the richest person in the United States in 2012?[2] Yup, Bill Gates of Microsoft. Without the software brain, a PC is just a box of plastic and wires. But Bill Gates made Microsoft *the* platform by which PCs could communicate. This is beginning to change due to open systems such as Linux and other all-in-one communication devices, including smartphones. For Mac devotees, just remember that Apple has at most 8 percent of the PC market share. Let's just say that Bill Gates and Microsoft are, for the time being, doing just fine. If a product or service is unique, then its suppliers can exert power.

Costs of switching are high. Did you sign a contract when you purchased your cell phone? Did it stipulate something along the lines that if you switched providers within a two-year period, you would be on the hook for $200? If so, you experienced supplier power due to high costs of switching. Similarly, your company may be at the mercy of its supplier if changing over to another supplier involves significant expenses. These expenses can be in the form of having to reformulate ingredients, reconfigure manufacturing processes, or redesign packaging and promotional materials.

Substitutions are few or none. You may be able to mitigate supplier power if you can obtain different products or services that satisfy similar needs. For example, if one of your food products' main ingredients is cane sugar, you may be able to switch to another form of sugar, say beet sugar. You may even consider artificial sweeteners. However, if few or no substitutes exist, and your company depends on the input, then you will find yourself at the mercy of suppliers.

Forward integration is possible. HTC is one of the largest smartphone vendors in the United States. But you may not have heard of it—yet. That's because HTC, a Taiwanese contract manufacturer, made phones for PC companies such as Compaq.[3] In this way, it remained invisible, until two years ago. Management at HTC realized that they could enter into the smartphone market with their own "HTC" brand. By engaging in this so-called forward integration, HTC now competes head-on with other smartphone brands, including Apple. As a strategist, you want to keep in mind the potential risk of your suppliers coming into your space and competing directly with you.

They have multiple end markets. Car parts manufacturers only have one end market they can supply: the automotive industry. This means that the car parts manufacturer is wholly dependent on what happens in that particular industry. If the market sours, as it did during the 2008 recession when consumers stopped buying cars, manufacturers are left at the mercy of their buyers, including their customers such as GM and Chrysler. (How would you have liked to be a supplier to either of these companies, both of which went belly-up in 2009?) Now take plastic packaging suppliers. The end markets these manufacturers serve, or potentially can serve, are almost limitless: toys, food, beverages, electronics, pharmaceuticals, etc. If certain end markets become unattractive, they simply shift their efforts elsewhere. In this way, the availability of more end markets gives suppliers more power to be choosy.

Buyer Power

Just like your suppliers, your buyers too can work against you. The saying "the customer is always right" suggests that you should bend to your customers' will at all costs. That's completely false! What about customers who don't pay you? Or those who ask for too many concessions? Indeed, your buyers can turn into a liability when they become too demanding, with those demands costing you profitability. Let's look at some scenarios in which buyers can put the squeeze on you. Buyers are powerful when:

They buy in large quantities. Think of the punch card in your wallet or purse: buy ten cups of coffee, get the eleventh for free. If you're a good customer, meaning that you make frequent or large purchases, you come to expect favorable treatment. In the case of buyers, this favorable treatment translates into volume discounts. The Walmart example in Workshop 3 served to illustrate this idea. For the retailer to continue to sell huge volumes of everyday products at "everyday low prices," it squeezes its suppliers for price concessions, often down to a mere penny. Add up all those pennies, and you're talking real money!

Products are standard or undifferentiated. If you offer the same exact product or service as your competitor, what do you think will be the deciding factor for a purchaser? Price, of course. Indeed, a buyer can and will play competitors off each other until one player gives up. That said, as you'll see later, one way to make an undifferentiated product stand out is through great customer service. But in that case, the service becomes the differentiator.

Quality is less important. A friend of ours once bought a pair of sneakers with an (almost) unnoticeable scratch for 80 percent off the retail price. He was going to break them in shortly, so he knew that they were going to get a lot more scuff marks in no time. In this instance, because the visual quality of the shoe was secondary, our friend was able to get a great deal. Similarly, companies willing to trade off quality for "good enough" products and services are in a better position to bargain.

Buyers earn low profits. If buyers make little money to begin with, as is the case in the grocery business (you're hitting it out of the ballpark if your net profit margin is over 2 percent!), they'll be motivated to grow that margin by saving a nickel here, a dime there. As a consequence, suppliers will often bear the brunt of these cost-cutting initiatives. You'll get an even better sense of this in the next workshop.

Backward integration is possible. How has Target managed not only to survive but to thrive in competition with a giant like Walmart? "Tarjay," as it is sometimes referred to, caters to a different consumer segment: those looking for a more fun and stylish, yet still affordable, shopping experience. To deliver on this promise to its customers, Target hires famous fashion designers like Mossimo and Isaac Mizrahi to design apparel, furniture, and dishware exclusively for the retailer.[4] This means that Target has "backward integrated" from a retailer who simply sells goods from manufacturers such as Nike, Levi's, and Fruit of the Loom to one that designs and makes its own branded products. Of course, this means that Target-designed jeans compete head-on with those made by Levi's, but hey, Target gets the sale either way, whether the customer buys its brand or the competitor's.

Threat of Substitutes

When trying to identify competitive forces that can erode your profitability, you want to think beyond your direct competitors' product offerings. Sure, if you own a burger joint, your customers can spend their dollars at McDonald's, Burger King, Sonic Burger, and so forth. Or if they're not in the mood for a burger, they might head over to Taco Bell or grab a slice of pizza. But they may also decide to go home and make themselves a sandwich, or they might simply decide to skip a meal. These options are substitutes, or products (and services) that are different but nevertheless satisfy similar needs and wants. For example, you may find that overall price increases to your category of products in the entire industry will drive your customers to look for cheaper substitutes in another industry.

Take e-mail as an example. Let's say that tomorrow morning, you wake up to find that your e-mail provider is going to start charging you a monthly service fee of $1,000. You immediately look around for an alternative e-mail provider (Gmail, Hotmail, Yahoo, AOL, etc.), but alas, they have all decided to charge the outrageous fee. What do you do? Well, e-mail is a form of communication, so you would look to other products and services that allow you to correspond. These include Facebook, texting, phone calls, and fax. Heck, you may even find yourself picking up a pen and a piece of paper and relying on good old snail mail. This so-called product-for-product substitution (meaning one "product" for another rather than one "brand" for another) helps you think through potential threats to not just your own product/service offerings, but also those to your entire industry.

You can also expand this conceptual thinking to even more generic substitutions. Going to the movies falls under the general category of entertainment and relaxation. So instead of spending $10 at the local cineplex, you might choose to go bowling instead. Or maybe you want to head over to Starbucks and read a magazine while sipping on a chai latte. Alternatively, you might save your $10 and simply go for a relaxing walk. (Just to keep things straight for you: if you chose one movie over another at the cineplex, that would represent direct competition for the movie studios. Renting a DVD or watching television at home would be more of a product-for-product substitution.)

In some cases, there are substitutions of products and services that consumers can simply do without. In the United States, cigarette companies are seeing fewer and fewer smokers, due both to health concerns and costs. So these companies are taking their business elsewhere, especially in emerging markets, where smoking is still on the rise.

Another substitution is "channel" substitution: Where else can your customers get the product? The book you're reading, for example, could have been purchased at a bookstore. But you also could have bought either a physical copy or a digital copy online. These all represent different point-of-sale and delivery channels that compete against each other. Believing that the electronic book would eventually replace the physical book, Amazon introduced the Kindle to try to manage the transition from one channel to the other.

Rivalry

Alright, now that we've covered four indirect competitive threats, we can turn to the last competitive force: rivalry. This is what most people usually think of as direct competition: Coke versus Pepsi, Toyota versus Ford, Boeing versus Airbus. The competitive issues involved usually concern which company offers either the cheaper or the more innovative products or services. Who is outspending whom in terms of marketing and advertising? Who has more sales? And so on. Answers to these questions can certainly give you a sense of how you stack up against some of your rivals. But they won't tell you the attractiveness of the industry in terms of its profit potential. In other words, even though you may find that your company performs well against your opponents, the overall industry could be in decline or even heading the way of the dinosaur. By standing back a bit to focus on certain industry factors, you can get a clearer picture of the level of competition in your industry. These factors include the following:

Number and size of competitors. Certainly competition increases, the more players enter the field. But you also want to pay heed to the size of the players. If competitors are roughly all the same size, with no apparent leader to establish industry practices, the intensity among rivals goes up. Take the airline industry. Over the past two decades, United, Delta, American, and Southwest, among the bigger players, have been duking it out in the skies, hoping to be profitable on a good day. More recently, these players have been buying their smaller competitors (Delta bought Northwest, United snapped up Continental, and American and US Airways are contemplating a merger) in an effort to become the dominant airline.[5]

Industry growth. If the industry's overall sales are not growing—that is, if the overall industry "pie" isn't growing—then competitors will start eyeing each other's slices to acquire growth. This is known as a *market share game* in technical terms and involves competitors engaging in heavy promotions and price cuts in efforts to dislodge customer loyalty.

Differentiation among products/services. As in the case of buyer power, where low differentiation in products and services causes purchasing decisions to be based on price, when rivals offer nearly identical products or services, and the costs for buyers to switch among rivals are low, the competition heats up. Consider, for example, commodity products such as grain or basic metals. Companies offering the same commodity will end up fighting tooth and nail over pennies.

Level of fixed costs. Think of a greeting card manufacturer. In this business, fixed costs are those expenses that have to be paid no matter how many greeting cards are produced: utilities, rent, insurance, etc. On the other hand, the more greeting cards you produce, the more paper and ink you need, right? Those are variable costs, because they fluctuate with the production volume. Industries that have high levels of fixed costs, such as chemical manufacturers, paper producers, and, yes, airlines, commonly will experience intense competition. Even as purchases slow and volume (or seats occupied) decrease competitors will keep the machines running so they can make payments to keep office lights on.

Barriers to exit. Just as some industries require less effort to enter than others, some are easier to exit. Someone making a living off an online newsletter only has to shut down the Web site to leave the industry. But consider shipyard companies seeking to quit the industry. It will be quite costly to disassemble the shipyard (e.g., cranes, slipways, dry docks) and to satisfy the environmental issues associated with the exit. Moreover, the equipment used in shipyards is specialized for shipbuilding, so the only buyer for this stuff is another shipbuilder. So, even if the shipbuilding/repair industry is in a slump, shipyard companies will operate at a loss rather than pay the exit fees. In turn, with shipyards already operating at a loss or breaking even at best, rivalry increases.

Product perishability. Have you ever bought day-old bagels? Sure, they're a bit hard, but you can't beat the 50 percent discount off the price of fresh bagels! The point is that competitors working with highly perishable products engage in stiff price competition to move product before it becomes stale. Product perishability applies not only to food products, but also to technologies. Personal computers, cell phones, and gaming consoles quickly lose value as new models displace old ones. Perishability can also apply to services. For example, certain travel sites offer steep discounts on flights, hotel rooms, and car rentals whose occupancies are about to expire.

Diversity of strategies. As should be apparent by now, industries whose participants only compete on price experience intense competition. On the other hand, when competitors take up different generic strategies (e.g., focused differentiator, differentiator, focused cost leader, cost leader) to distinguish themselves, the rivalry decreases. As long as players carve out their little spots in the sandbox and avoid bumping into each other, the industry's profit potential can remain intact.

As you conduct your Five Forces analysis, highlight those factors relating to each force that can be most troublesome to your business. You may want to use a simple rating system of low, medium, and high to designate the strength of factors and, by extension, the forces. Keep in mind that the stronger the Five Forces are collectively, the weaker the profit potential in the industry is. Once you have completed the first step of establishing the competitive dynamics in your industry, you can then move on step two: positioning your company to lessen those forces. The movie theater example in the next section will show you how.

Strategy in Action: The Movie Theater Industry

Scenario: You have just arrived at your family's picnic. It's the annual family affair that lets you reconnect with your aunts, uncles, cousins, and distant relatives. You're about to jump in line to grab a burger, when your Uncle Joey pulls you aside. He's eager to share with you, the strategic thinker in the family, his latest business venture and to get your objective guidance. Your stomach is grumbling for food, but alas, you surrender yourself and your services. The two of you grab a park bench away from the crowd. Uncle Joey leans in to reveal his big idea. He's been eyeing the downtown movie theater that's been sitting empty and abandoned for a good five years. He can get it on the cheap, he says, and plans to renovate it and bring it back to its former splendor and beauty. "Whatta ya think?" Uncle Joey's question activates your strategic muscle, kicking off a two-step analysis of the movie industry and Uncle Joey's chances therein.

As we highlighted previously, the first step involves understanding the overall profit potential of the movie industry. Once we have a firm grasp on the forces that chip away at the industry's profitability, we can move to the second step to see if we can in fact position ourselves favorably to mitigate those forces.

Threat of new entrants. How difficult or easy is it to get into the movie theater business? Entering the market at the local level, as Uncle Joey intends to do, seems relatively affordable. Costs include purchasing or leasing a property and, with a little bit of elbow grease, renovating the movie house. Given the viewership volume, however, one-location, independent movie theaters don't realize significant economies of scale or scope. In addition, though each movie is unique, the actual product "format" is largely undifferentiated; the *Iron Man 3* movie you watch in theaters is the same that you eventually see on DVD or Netflix. Besides basic business licenses and insurance, no additional government regulations stand in the way of opening the doors to the movie theater. That said, at the level of a local, one-location, independent movie theater, the potential to generate revenue will be rather limited: Will viewers come to the theater? If so, on which days of the week? If the theater can show only one movie at a time, how often will you need to introduce a new release? Will the new release actually draw a crowd?

As the scale of the movie theater business increases, so do the costs. That is, competing on a nationwide basis with a chain of movie houses à la Regal, Carmike, or Cinemark will cost a boatload to scope out, buy or lease, equip, and staff the theaters. Entering the movie theater business on a broad basis will bring economies of scale (imagine the materials and equipment needed to build 1,300 theaters versus one) and economies of scope (showing multiple movies concurrently and selling gazillion-dollar soda and popcorn to viewers). What quickly becomes apparent is that though it may not cost much to enter the business on a small scale, the profit potential is also limited at that particular level. As the scale (number of theaters) and scope (geographic footprint) of the business increase, the threat of new entrants decreases dramatically.

Buyer power. The buyers in the movie theater industry are the viewers. How often do you go to the movies? You may be a movie buff and go a few times a month. Other folks will go a few times a year. That said, there are few incentives for regular moviegoers in terms of price concessions. And given the ever-increasing cost of tickets, some moviegoers will become price-sensitive. As just mentioned, the actual product, the movie, is undifferentiated, with little to lock in a moviegoer to the relationship with the movie theater. That is, the moviegoer doesn't incur any costs for switching among different movie theater chains. As such, customers may start looking around for cheaper fare at other theaters or even opt to go to lower-priced matinees. Can moviegoers backward integrate? In terms of the movie product, movie studios are now beginning to offer in-theater releases concurrently on Amazon.com. Aside from the legal means to backward integrate, Web sites that offer pirated movies have proliferated over the past decade. In terms of the movie theater "experience," consumers can and do build sophisticated entertainment centers in their homes. Taken together, the power that buyers can exert on movie theaters is quite extensive.

Supplier power. The suppliers in the movie theater industry are the film studios. Currently, over 50 percent of wide-release movies are produced by just four studios: Sony's Columbia Pictures, Warner Brothers, Disney, and Comcast's Universal Pictures. Going down the list of what makes suppliers powerful, we can check off most of them: there are more buyers than suppliers; the product content (i.e., the movie) is unique; and for movie theaters to forego the movies from one film studio means they may miss out on a potential blockbuster, a form of switching cost. We will shortly examine why the threat of substitutes for the movie theater experience is high, but for the actual film is low: watching movies in some form or fashion is an important part of people's entertainment routine. And although film studios are unlikely to forward integrate into the movie theater business, as noted in the discussion on buyer power, they have multiple end markets in which to sell their products, including online, cable, and DVD rental. These forms of supplier power can destabilize the profit potential of movie theaters.

Threat of substitutes. How do you access movies other than at the movie theater? The answer is through cable, satellite, online video-on-demand services, and DVD rentals. You access them at home, at a friend's place, or in a hotel. These all represent channel substitutes, because the content of the movie can be accessed and viewed through different channels. In some cases, viewers may prefer these channels to the movie theater—there is no need to put up with that annoying person who doesn't turn off his smartphone! Beyond channel substitutes, product substitutes also exist. Instead of going to see a movie, folks may choose to hunker down and watch a miniseries at home or a sports event at a bar. Generic substitutes involve other forms of entertainment that divert consumer dollars away from movie theaters: attending a concert, going out to a restaurant, reading a book or magazine over a cup of coffee at Starbucks. Finally, because going to the movies isn't a necessity, consumers can simply choose to go without. The high substitution threat for movie theaters makes for fierce pressure on the industry's profit potential.

Rivalry. Regal Entertainment and AMC Entertainment are the two largest movie theater chain operators in the United States, together accounting for over $6 billion—or 40 percent—of the $15 billion movie theater industry.[6] Whereas the top four companies account for over 60 percent of the industry's market, the remainder still consists of independent movie theaters. Growth rates for the industry are nominal at best—just over 1 percent per year—which means that large rivals are eyeing each other's piece of the pie.[7] For the most part, it's difficult to tell the movie theater operators apart once you find yourself inside the theater. The draw, first and foremost, is the movie currently being shown, although as we note in the second step of our analysis, operators such as IMAX provide a unique experience. As competitors have been scrambling to update their infrastructure, from digital and 3-D projectors to surround-sound systems and plush seating, both the fixed costs and the barriers to exit have gone up. This means that even in a slump, such as during the most recent recession, movie theater operators will hang in there, even operating at a loss in the hope of an eventual turnaround. Finally, the movie theater industry reflects a wide diversity of strategies. There are differentiators such as Regal, cost leaders such as Carmike Cinemas, focused differentiators including IMAX, and focused cost leaders including old-school drive-ins. Degree of rivalry? High!

Silence. Uncle Joey looks as if he's been doused in ice-cold water. What he thought was a no-brainer actually carries with it a slew of challenges and risks. Trying to save the sliver of enthusiasm he had twenty minutes ago, Uncle Joey asks if there are ways to possibly squeeze out a profit from this investment. Here's where the science ends and the art takes over.

For a single-venue, independent movie theater, competing head-on against the national chains will be impossible. The Regals and Cinemarks of the world try to capitalize on first-release mainstream movies, drawing in the crowds who want to see the latest blockbuster on a big screen with the latest and greatest technology. With that option closed to Uncle Joey, he may want to pick a different product, such as screening hard-to-get independent or art-house films to a select audience. He may also consider rescreening classics, although these are also widely available through the substitute channels. To differentiate an undifferentiated product, he could focus on the customer experience, including customer service, by offering customers a more extensive and even healthy food option, alcoholic beverages for adults, and sofa seating. To make the moviegoing experience just part of the evening's outing, he may partner with vendors such as bars, restaurants, and clubs that can offer an entire evening's entertainment to a customer. All of these options lower the Five Forces to some extent and increase the overall profit potential for Uncle Joey's foray into the movie theater business. Now, whether he still wants to move forward on the opportunity, given the risks and potential returns, is up to him. Time for that burger.

Workshop Takeaway

We introduced you to the forces and relevant factors that can make your industry attractive or unattractive in terms of its profitability. As you'll find out in applying this powerful framework, each industry has its own unique characteristics that make it more or less competitive. Keep in mind that as you go through the Five Forces analysis, some forces (and factors that determine the extent of those forces) will be more significant than others in dictating the extent of competition, so make sure to identify the most critical ones. Remember, the Five Forces analysis is a two-step approach! This means that you begin to think about ways to mitigate or lower competitive forces for your firm only once you have a clear understanding of the overall industry's profit patterns.

The Value System: Who's Kicking—and Kissing—Whom?

With a clear picture of the forces that can potentially undermine your ability to turn a profit, you can begin to find ways to weaken those forces and boost your profitability. Two forces that require an additional level of consideration are buyer power and supplier power. After all, you may have multiple suppliers (of, e.g., raw materials, subcomponents, and components) and buyers (end-product manufacturers, wholesalers, retailers, etc.). This is where the value system comes in, a very handy tool also conceptualized by Michael Porter.[1] The value system allows you to map out all the industry participants that help bring a product or service to market. Think of the value system as a river. Along that river, there are numerous docks where participants help build the ship (the product or service) as it heads downstream toward its final destination, the customer. In this analogy, the docks along the river consist of upstream suppliers (of wood, sails, construction and assembly, etc.) and downstream channels (testing, tugboat assistance, etc.) and buyers. You may be saying to yourself, "This sounds an awful lot like a supply chain!" Indeed, there are similarities when mapping out the industry participants. However, the main difference is that a value system focuses first and foremost on the value added to the product or service as it comes to market. In other words, it allows you to determine how an industry's revenues and profits spread out across the participants: Who's the most important player? Who's making the big bucks, and why? Which companies represent a potential bottleneck for us? Which companies have the muscle to kick us? In turn, which companies do we have to play nice with ("kiss") to stay in business?

But wait, it doesn't end there. The value system is much more dynamic! An additional benefit to conducting a value system analysis is that we can also figure out if an industry's revenues and profits are being displaced over time. Indeed, as industries evolve, some more quickly than others, new profit opportunities arise while old ones disappear. This means that you should never take existing value systems for granted. Instead, try to think of ways to loosen the chokehold of some players through a variety of strategic moves, which we'll cover shortly. Finally, if you think outside the box, you may even conceive of entirely *new* value systems that will afford you more control and profitability.

Let's begin with a visual of the value system map. Figure 5.1 shows the river with upstream suppliers and downstream channels and buyers, with the Firm representing your company under analysis.

Keep in mind that there are often multiple suppliers, channels, and buyers, so you need to lay out these participants in their correct order by indicating who's supplying whom, who's buying from whom, and so forth.

You'll recall that in the previous workshop, we touched on Microsoft's supplier power in the personal computer industry. To get a more in-depth understanding of Microsoft's position in the industry as well as its power over manufacturers dependent on its operating system, take a look at the detailed value system of the PC industry (figure 5.2).

Beginning on the left, you'll see the raw materials providers. These are suppliers of plastic resin, copper wiring, silicone, and so forth. Next come the subcomponent and component suppliers, who add value by actually making the cabling and wiring, injected-molded parts like keys for the keyboard and the mouse, the printed circuit boards, and so forth, as well as the more assembled components: the CPU, the power supply (a fancy word for battery), the thermal management system that keeps your notebook from overheating, the digital display (a fancy word for screen), and so on. The electronics assembly provider is also known as electronics manufacturing services, although "manufacturing" is a misnomer, because these companies don't make anything. Similarly, the original equipment manufacturers (OEMs), such as Dell, Toshiba, Sony, Acer, HP, and Lenovo, don't manufacture their products. In fact, they hardly touch them. Instead, today's OEMs focus primarily on designing the next generation of laptops,

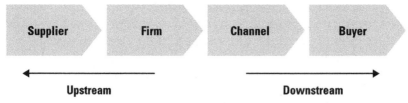

Figure 5.1. The Value System

Figure 5.2. Value System: The Personal Computer Industry

desktops, tablets, and so on, then selling them through direct (their own Web sites) and indirect (retailer) channels.

Why place the software developers *after* the OEMs, you might be asking yourself? Sure, Microsoft supplies its operating system *to* the OEMs, who then ship the final product. However, from a value-added perspective, Microsoft is placed onto the hardware product. As mentioned in a previous workshop, without the operating system, or the brains, a PC is simply a box of plastic and wires. Furthermore, when considering PCs, consumers have numerous options in brands, but only two options when it comes to operating systems: Microsoft or Apple. In doing this kind of analysis, we can see why Microsoft traditionally held so much power in the PC value system.

So what's currently happening in the PC value system? Well, over the past decade, it has become increasingly volatile due to technological evolutions.[2] For starters, the Internet itself has become one giant operating system. Consumers can now download applications and upload documents directly through Google, for example. Moreover, as we all become less reliant on PCs and more on smartphones, tablets, and interactive televisions, there is less need for Microsoft's Windows operating systems and productivity software tools. With the downstream buyer demand for PCs dwindling, Microsoft is losing its clout. And while the company is racing to keep up with and even leapfrog some of the technological innovations, to what extent it'll ever be able to regain its dominance remains highly uncertain.

Once you have a strong grasp on what your particular value system looks like, you can begin to strategize ways to enhance your competitive positioning within it. In the next few sections, we provide strategies relating to vertical integration and horizontal diversification.

Vertical Integration

The core concept of vertical integration is quite simple: Are you going to take responsibility for making a particular product or service, or are you going to let someone else do it?[3] In the previous example of the PC value system, the tasks of creating the hardware and the software belong to two disparate industry participants: the OEMs and the software developers. However, Apple is a different story. Since its inception, Apple has created both the hardware *and* the software. In this way, Apple is said to be *vertically integrated.*

Companies taking on additional tasks in the current value system can vertically integrate either backward or forward. Backward integration involves heading upstream in the value system to take on additional responsibilities, whereas forward integration involves going downstream. A few examples will help to clarify the difference:

Forward integration: Let's stick with Apple. Prior to 2001, Apple's products were sold largely through big-box computer and electronics stores such as Circuit City and CompUSA. In 2001, however, Apple opened the first Apple Store, in McLean, Virginia, dedicated solely to selling Apple-related products.[4] In doing so, Apple forward integrated into owning and operating its own retail stores. Why did Apple get into retailing? Simply put, Apple realized it wasn't getting the care and attention it deserved from the big-box retailers. Indeed, if you've ever been around MacHeads (die-hard Apple fans), you've probably noticed that they see Apple's offerings not just as products but rather as a reflection and extension of their digital lifestyle. Apple Stores allow the company to control the shopper's experience at point of purchase and to set an expectation of what it means to be part of the cult of Mac: you are modern, fashionable, a minimalist, and at the forefront of the technological revolution.

Backward integration: In spring 2012, Delta Air Lines bought an oil refinery.[5] Yup, imagine a company whose primary purpose is to fly people and their luggage from Point A to Point B getting into the business of transforming crude oil into petroleum. At first glance, this backward integration (i.e., going upstream to the fuel source of the airline industry) seems, well, bizarre. However, consider an airline's largest expenses: labor and fuel. They can't cut more staff, largely due to union contracts, so acquiring a fuel source allows for some control over costs. Indeed, it didn't take long for analysts covering Delta Airlines to come around to this strategic move.

Benefits of Vertical Integration

The previous two examples are illustrative of the strategic benefits afforded to companies engaging in vertical integration. Specifically, a company can gain better control of its value system and at times also capture more of the profit pie within that value system. Furthermore, vertical integration allows a company to build up barriers that can put existing competitors at a disadvantage or even keep new competitors from entering the industry. By purchasing the oil refinery, Delta can lock out competitors from that particular source of fuel. Of course Delta can decide to sell some of its fuel to its competitors at a nice mark-up, which will provide it with an added bonus: in addition to lowering its cost structure, the company also creates a new revenue stream!

Risks of Vertical Integration

You need to take into account the possible risks of backward or forward integration. For one thing, moves or acquisitions upstream or downstream can be expensive. In both the Apple and Delta examples, these vertical integration moves were quite costly, without any upfront assurances that they would work. Moreover, risk exists when venturing into parts of a value system that a company is operationally and strategically unfamiliar with. Certainly Delta Air Lines has a firm understanding of the airline business, but what does it know about running a refinery? It'll be a steep learning curve for its executives to learn the ins and outs of this acquisition. Finally, in taking on more control in a value system, a company can become less flexible and responsive to changes that arise in its particular value system. For instance, during the 1990s cell phone operator Sprint built its own cellular network using one type of wireless standard (CDMA, for you techies who want to know). Although this helped the telecommunications player build its initial presence in a highly competitive marketplace, it eventually ended up working against it, as the network failed to keep up with the evolution of cell phones.[6] As bandwidth-hungry smartphones gained acceptance with consumers, Sprint's vertical integration of building and running its own CDMA network caused customers to migrate to competitors such as AT&T and Verizon. Indeed, Sprint couldn't make the popular iPhone available on its network until a full four years after Apple introduced it![7]

Alternatives to Vertical Integration

Vertical integration is not an all-or-nothing strategic decision. Rather, there are less expensive ways to capture control of and/or decrease fluctuations and uncertainties of a value system. You could, for instance, negotiate preferred supplier contracts that ensure you'll have access to and delivery of certain products and services in the future. Preferred vendor contracts, on the other hand, may favor certain vendors because they can move more product through the value system. A strategic alliance is a further step, in which two organizations pool resources to create new products, processes, distribution channels, promotional opportunities, and so forth.[8] The alliance between United Airlines and Starbucks Coffee Company fits this bill. United provides Starbucks with another channel for distribution, whereas Starbucks allows United to differentiate its in-air service by offering premium coffee to its travelers.

If a strategic alliance is a dating period between two companies, then a joint venture is more like an engagement. Things become a bit more serious. Firms entering into a joint venture make a pact to create a new entity, with each party contributing capital, personnel, and other resources. In forming a joint venture, the time and resource investments are greater than in a strategic alliance; in fact, both parties stand to gain and lose much more from their partnership as they jointly manage the operation and share in its profits and losses.[9] As is often the case with partnerships, squabbles can arise about who put in more money, who's more dedicated, who's carrying more of the load, and so on. In fact, the numbers show that a majority of joint ventures dissolve within a decade.[10]

Horizontal Diversification

If vertical integration involves moving up and down the value system, then horizontal diversification concerns expansion at the same level of the value system into more or less similar products or services.[11] Let's revisit the visual representation of the value system and indicate what, exactly, horizontal diversification entails.

Suppose that a company makes Product A. In this case, the product is cigarettes. Tough business these days, considering the product's health risks, the backlash against tobacco companies, and legislation to curb smoking (e.g., smoking bans, purchase restrictions, cigarette taxes). To mitigate some of the risks in this industry and combat its overall domestic decline, the company acquires a manufacturer of chewing tobacco products. The value system remains quite similar, given that cigarettes and chewing tobacco have similar inputs (e.g., tobacco) and distribution channels (grocery stores, gas stations, etc.). Of course the company's executives will have to learn something new about the chewing tobacco business, but this horizontal diversification allows the company to add a related product without drastically changing its business. Figure 5.3 depicts the company's addition of Product B and its placement in the value system.

Companies choosing to diversify horizontally can do so through either internal or external means. Internal horizontal diversification involves expansion at the same level of the value system through a company's own

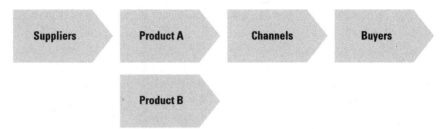

Figure 5.3. Horizontal Diversification

initiatives in research and development, innovation, new product launches, and so forth. That is, the company uses its in-house resources to organically grow into a related market. In contrast, companies pursuing external horizontal diversification rely on mergers, acquisitions, joint ventures, and strategic alliances to enter related markets. The following examples should help to illustrate the two avenues to horizontal diversification.

Internal horizontal diversification: Japanese automotive giant Honda broke into the U.S. market in the late 1950s.[12] However, the product initially offered to the U.S. consumer was not an automobile, but a motorcycle—actually, a 50-cc moped. The Honda Super Cub 50 offered consumers, especially youngsters, a fun and inexpensive way to get around town. For the next decade, Honda successfully grew market share and in the process built a brand and a reputation for affordability and reliability. It was only in 1970 that management felt the timing was right to introduce the American consumer to its automobile, the N600 model. As they say, the rest is history. In this particular case, however, the horizontal diversification was internally driven and developed as Honda expanded its means of transportation from motorcycles to automobiles.

External horizontal diversification: The previously discussed example of the cigarette manufacturer acquiring a chewing tobacco company did, in fact, happen. In late 2008, Altria Group, parent company of cigarette giant Phillip Morris USA, purchased US Smokeless Tobacco Company (UST), maker of Copenhagen and Skoal chewing tobacco, for approximately $10 billion.[13] In deciding to add (via acquisition in the external market) rather than make (through internal research, development, and manufacturing) these smokeless tobacco products, Altria instantly added a number of established and profitable brands to its lineup of tobacco products.

Benefits of Horizontal Diversification

As the previous examples suggest, horizontal diversification provides companies with a number of advantages. For one thing, expanding into related products or services can bring additional economies of scale and scope. In the case of Altria buying UST, because Altria is simply adding tobacco-based products, its increased volume in purchases from existing suppliers will afford the company even steeper discounts (e.g., economies of scale). Similarly, you'll recall that economies of scope involve efficiencies a company reaps from selling a wider range of products than just a handful, especially when the distribution channels are already established. With Copenhagen and Skoal in its portfolio, Altria can simply push those products through its existing cigarette distributors. In addition to gaining scale and scope economies, companies pursuing horizontal diversification can also sidestep volatility in their existing value system.

Risks of Horizontal Diversification

By now, you've noticed that for every strategic pro, there exists a con. In the case of horizontal diversification, integrating expanded product or service lines can be a tricky affair. Management may not have the product, marketing, or sales know-how, even if the expansion is related to the core business. Furthermore, the synergies anticipated from the diversification, including economies of scale and scope, may take longer to realize, or they may not materialize at all. Externally driven horizontal diversification, especially through acquisitions and mergers, can be especially problematic. First, even though the acquirer may have conducted effective due diligence (a fancy term for "looking under the hood"), there are bound to be surprises (e.g., accounting discrepancies, bad customer accounts, environmental issues) in the company it purchases. Second, combining cultures from two disparate companies is probably the biggest challenge. Issues of "that's not how we've done it in the past" or "our products are so much better than theirs" can throw a monkey wrench into the assimilation process. And, indeed, the proof is in the pudding. The majority of mergers and acquisitions fail to bring the intended synergies and profits to the combined entities.[14]

Other Approaches to Horizontal Diversification

Pursuing horizontal diversification does not have to be a binary decision: internal or external. Instead, there are intermediate steps available to allow a company to balance the potential risks and rewards involved in the expansion. These include co-branding and bundling. When co-branding, a company might simply dip its toe into a related market by partnering with another firm already in that particular market. To illustrate, think about Tabasco. Yes, the hot sauce. You may have come across some of the company's co-branding initiatives, including Tabasco-flavored Spam, Tabasco-flavored Cheez-It Crackers, and even Tabasco-flavored pickles from Vlasic! Now, Tabasco probably isn't contemplating getting into the cracker or pickle business by itself, but these opportunities allow the hot sauce maker to expand its brand into heretofore uncharted territory. One co-branding opportunity is of particular interest: Heinz "Hot & Spicy" Ketchup with Tabasco. For both of these companies, this co-branding affords an opportunity to test-drive spicy ketchup before jumping into the market. And indeed, both Heinz and McIlhenny (the company behind Tabasco) now have their *own* lines of spicy ketchup.

In a bundling relationship, two or more companies decide to package and sell their complementary products together. The best-known example is your PC or desktop that comes loaded with various software programs. So when you fire up your newly purchased HP or Dell laptop, you might find trial offers for Norton AntiVirus, QuickBooks, Adobe Reader, and of course, the Microsoft Office suite. You may even have come across bundled products at some of your local eateries. Make your sandwich order a meal, and they'll throw in a drink and a bag of chips. And if you're lucky, a cookie.

Finally, as in the case of vertical integration, strategic alliances and joint ventures also offer alternatives to committing fully to horizontal diversification. Companies can enter into a strategic alliance to explore related markets. This was the case with food marketer B&G Foods and Crock-Pot manufacturer Jarden Corporation, which entered into a strategic alliance in spring 2012 to create a line of Crock-Pot seasoning mixes.[15] B&G brings its know-how in producing foods and condiments, while Jarden contributes its leading position and brand as "The Original Slow Cooker." On the other hand, beer giants SABMiller and Molson Coors, in creating the MillerCoors joint venture in 2007, pooled their production and distribution know-how in efforts to compete more effectively against their archrival, Anheuser-Busch.[16]

Strategy in Action: Amazon and the Kindle

In fall 2007, electronic commerce giant Amazon.com launched its electronic book (e-book) reader, the Kindle. A few other companies, including Sony, already had e-book readers on the consumer market, but it was Amazon's Kindle that cracked open the market and became the dominant player, at least for the immediate future. In doing so, Amazon extended its assault on the value system of traditional book publishing, in the process gaining additional control among its upstream suppliers and downstream channels and buyers. To get a clearer understanding of this progression, we will walk you through Amazon's disruptive impact in the book publishing value system since its founding in the mid-1990s. We'll begin by revisiting the publishing industry's value system prior to the Internet and e-commerce. Tracking Amazon's progression from e-commerce pioneer to e-book revolutionary, you will see that the value system and its participants have been completely transformed, to the benefit of some and the detriment of others, and even to the demise of an unlucky few.

Pre-1990s

Figure 5.4 shows the book publishing value system prior to the commercialization of the Internet in the mid-1990s. Upstream, all the way to the left, is the content provider, or the author, who conceives of the idea for a book and writes it. The traditional course of action, pre-Internet, was for the author to approach the agent with a few sample chapters and a proposal in the hope of getting agent representation. The agent, in turn, worked on behalf of the author to shop the manuscript around to various publishing houses in the hope of locking in a publishing contract. Once the manuscript was completed, the publisher prepped it for the market, editing and composing it, creating a cover design, marketing it, issuing press releases, and so forth. The next step was to forward the manuscript to the printer to print the physical book in hardcover, paperback, or both. The printer then passed on the completed book to the wholesaler, who distributed it to independent bookstores and book-retailing giants like Barnes & Noble. The retailer marked up the book to the retail price in the hope of selling it to the end consumer. All along the way, each participant in the value system took a piece of the action. The retailer received a markup on the wholesale price of the book. The wholesaler collected a markup from the publisher. The printer received a transaction fee based on the cost per copy and the volume of the print run. The publisher, agent, and author split the remainder of the price of the book; that is, after deducting the revenue from the retailer, wholesaler, and printer, the publisher, agent, and author all collected their respective cut on each book sold.

Figure 5.4. The Book Publishing Value System: Pre-Internet

Figure 5.5. The Book Publishing Value System: Enter Amazon

Amazon.com

Enter Jeff Bezos, founder of Amazon.com, in 1994. His intention at the time for his online bookseller was simple: present consumers with a wider variety of books through his Web site than could be offered through traditional brick-and-mortar stores. That is, whereas existing book retailers, both large and small, were limited by the number of shoppers walking into the store, as well as by the number of books they could physically stock in the store, Amazon.com could offer any title (available in print) to anyone, anywhere. Using a centralized warehouse, Amazon.com stocked a slew of book titles to fulfill shoppers' orders. If the title was unavailable, the company would find it elsewhere. When looking at the value system, you will notice that Amazon.com, in using the Web as its retail location, cut out the retailer, in the process capturing that value of the markup to the retailer for itself. By receiving orders directly from the consumer and subsequently shipping directly from the warehouse to the consumer, Amazon.com was in a position to sell books at a significantly lower price than brick-and-mortar stores could. Mind you, printers were still largely involved in the value system, because digital books had not yet appeared on the market. But you can already anticipate the ensuing disruption to the value system, as illustrated in figure 5.5.

The Kindle

Fast-forward to November 2007, when Amazon.com introduced its version of an e-reader, the Kindle. By then, the company was already the largest seller of books in the world, with a stranglehold on the publishing industry. While other companies had already been jockeying for position to establish leading share in the e-reader market, Amazon.com's sheer size and stature in the industry could force book publishers to do its bidding. Not only was the Kindle an overall better e-reader, but it also offered a much wider selection of titles for consumers to purchase. The Kindle quickly became the dominant e-reader in the market, with its popularity eroding the continued viability of book printers. Books no longer had to be physically printed. By cutting out printers in the value system, Amazon not only captured much of that value for itself, but also significantly

Figure 5.6. The Book Publishing Value System: Enter the Kindle

reduced its operating costs of having to physically store books in its warehouses. How the Kindle impacted the book publishing value system is represented in figure 5.6.

Acquisition of CreateSpace and Dorchester Books

The assault on the traditional book publishing value system continues. In the summer of 2012, Amazon.com acquired Dorchester Books, a publisher of children's books.[17] In doing so, it effectively became its own publishing house. And through the CreateSpace service, the online retailer today offers authors the opportunity to self-publish their books. In revisiting the value system, we can see how both of these initiatives closed the gap between the author and Amazon.com, in the process cutting out other value-adding players. Figure 5.7 depicts Amazon.com's current value system.

Our illustration of Amazon.com's value system does not suggest that agents, publishers, printers, and even retailers have ceased to exist. They still have a place in the industry, as long as you can find a physical book at your local bookstore, Barnes & Noble, or Walmart, as well as Amazon. That said, a value system analysis of the book publishing industry shows the astonishing extent of the upheaval this long-standing industry has experienced over the past two decades.

Figure 5.7. The Book Publishing Value System: Today

Workshop Takeaway

In this workshop, we familiarized you with the concept of the value system, what it represents, and how it can help you strategize your competitive position within your industry. By first mapping out the various participants, from upstream suppliers to downstream channels and buyers, the value system can help you identify where, in your industry, value and the related profits are being generated. Analyzing the value system also allows you to pinpoint which players or categories of players are doing the kicking in your industry. That is, which players represent a bottleneck to your ability to capture and secure more of your industry's profit potential? With that information under your belt, it becomes much clearer whether your company can bolster its competitive place in the value system through vertical integration, horizontal diversification, or both.

The Value Chain: The Ins and Outs of Your Business

The workshops up to this point have focused primarily on competitive elements in the external environment. Think about it. We started by identifying the so-called macros using SWOT. The generic strategies framework allows you to evaluate competitors' positioning in terms of broad-based or narrow-focused differentiation and cost leadership. We then moved to the Five Forces to get a handle on your industry's overall profit potential, to distinguish among competitive forces that can squeeze out your ability to make money, and to explore ways to protect against some of those forces. And the previous workshop on the value system introduced you to a handy tool for identifying your upstream suppliers and downstream channels and buyers, isolating potential chokepoints and finding ways to improve your position among those players.

Now it's time to get inside your company. In this workshop, we break down Michael Porter's value system into the value chain, thereby focusing on what happens *inside* the four walls of your company.[1] The importance of a value chain analysis is twofold. First, you need to understand how to organize your company and its various functions to achieve its strategic intent. Second, once you have a firm grasp on how you go about doing what you do to make a profit, you can then ask yourself *the* key question of strategy: Is there anything that makes my company different or unique? How you go about answering that question is covered in Workshop 7, where we get into core competencies.

So, you ask, what's a value chain? Well, if the value system depicts how an industry arranges itself for a product or service to come to market, then a value chain describes the activities a company must engage in to bring its products or services to market. Conceptually speaking, an organization is more than a random collection of people, buildings, machinery, funds, and so forth. Rather, it involves an organized (hence the "organization") system of interdependent activities. And depending on how well you, the strategist, set up and manage those activities, you can deliver value to your customers and, by extension, to your company.

Let's drive home this last point. You'll recall from the first workshop defining strategy that it involves being both operationally effective (i.e., performing similar activities better than competitors) and unique (performing different activities/performing similar activities differently). In doing a value chain analysis, you can begin to explore what those activities look like and how they can be arranged to achieve both operational effectiveness and uniqueness.

Start with your overall generic strategy and whether you intend to compete on cost or differentiation. Why? Because depending on the generic strategy you choose, the activities in the value chain will be tailored to that particular strategy. So, if the generic strategy is focused on trying to achieve cost leadership, then the value chain will need to emphasize making those activities as efficient and economical as possible. On the other hand, for a differentiation strategy, the company brings something unique to the market that can command a premium from customers. The following equations simplify this thinking:

Cost Leadership: Revenue – *Cost* = Profit Margin
Differentiation: *Revenue* – Cost = Profit Margin

In the cost leadership equation, the primary focus is on controlling costs. Since the product is undifferentiated and can't command a premium in the marketplace, the company's activities should be focused on managing the cost side of the ledger.

In the case of differentiation, the company's activities should be directed toward creating a unique product or service so that the customer will pay the premium, to garner a higher price point. That isn't to say that controlling costs is not important, but the priority is making something distinctive that customers cannot find elsewhere in the marketplace.

Take a look at the value chain in figure 6.1. At first glance, it has some similarities to the value system, especially because both have activities running from left to right. But what distinguishes one from the other is that the value chain focuses predominantly on the activities occurring inside the firm. These activities are broken into two categories: primary and support. And as just mentioned, how you manage those activities, individually and in unison, dictates the profit margin you can achieve.

Value Chain:

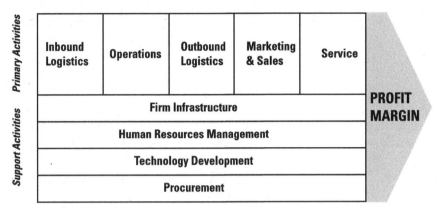

Figure 6.1. The Value Chain

Let's break down the primary and support activities and explore how they can inform your value chain analysis. For simplicity's sake, we're going to rely on a lemonade stand example again to describe all those activities. Your lemonade stand, for the time being, will serve freshly squeezed lemonade at, say, $2 a cup. Pricey? Ok, let's make the lemons organic to justify the expense. Compared to your competitors, who are making undifferentiated lemonade using powder and charging 50 cents a cup, you are going to position yourself as a differentiator.

Primary Activities

Primary activities are those within the company that contribute directly to the creation and delivery of a product or service to the customer. The five primary activities, in sequence, are inbound logistics, operations, outbound logistics, marketing and sales, and service.

Inbound logistics. This activity involves sourcing inputs in anticipation of production. That is, you are obtaining, receiving, warehousing, and preparing your resources to make your product. In the case of service firms, the resources often include the skills and talents of your employees, such as journalists at newspapers, industry experts in consulting, and lawyers in law firms. What comprises the inbound logistics for your lemonade stand? Well, as the adage goes, make lemonade when life gives you lemons, so you need lemons. And they have to be organically certified, no less! Apart from lemons, you'll also need a juicer, water, ice, sugar, a jug, cups, etc. Once you have checked off all the inputs on your list, you can move on to operations.

Operations. Here you are concerned with transforming the inputs (e.g., raw materials, components, intellectual capital) into a finished good. In the case of, say, a research firm, the finished good might be a research report that you can then sell into the market. At your lemonade stand, your operations are simply making lemonade: squeeze the lemons, then add water, ice, sugar, and so forth.

Outbound logistics. With operations complete, you can prepare to send the product or service into the market. This activity involves warehousing, order fulfillment, and delivery, including transportation. With the lemonade made, your outbound logistics include setting up your curbside table and bringing the lemonade from the kitchen to the table for delivery to the customer. To keep your lemonade cool and from spoiling in the summer heat, you might even run an extension cord to a small refrigerator next to your table.

Marketing and sales. If you build it, chances are they won't come unless you make them aware of it. This is where the marketing and sales activities come in. You need to identify your target customers and reach them through advertising and promotional activities. You also need to set your optimal price and then figure out how you're going to go about selling your product or service. Sometimes, direct sales to the customer may be the preferred option. At other times, you may go through value-added resellers, wholesalers, etc. For this, your value system analysis can help you explore various options. Although you're going to sell your lemonade directly to customers walking or driving by (and remember, you can even think through favorable positioning, as covered in Workshop 1), you will need to promote your $2-a-cup organic lemonade. For starters, you should post signs at the stand, as well as at either end of your street, so you can make passersby aware of your offerings. And while you're at it, it will probably help if you holler out, "Fresh organic lemonade . . . come get your fresh organic lemonade right here!!!"

Service. The last primary activity in your value chain is the customer service after the product or service is sold. This can range from a basic warranty to ongoing technical support and regular upgrades and maintenance. A bar of Hershey's chocolate will simply have a product warranty and a phone number in case you need to contact the company, whereas a printer from HP requires you to upload compatibility software and to find ways to purchase or refill printer cartridges. On a grander scale, an airplane manufacturer needs to have a network of maintenance and repair providers in place to service its airline customers with spare parts. Turning to your lemonade stand, part of your service component may include a simple "thank-you" to your customers. It's amazing how far that goes!

You can then offer a product guarantee, which can be especially important for freshly squeezed, organic lemonade, because the consistency can vary from one batch to the next. Finally, you may even incentivize your customers with a "get the next lemonade at half price" voucher to show your appreciation for their business.

Support Activities

To assist with the previously described primary activities, you want to turn your attention to a set of support activities. They provide you with an opportunity to consider important operational issues about your firm's culture, the kind of talent that you require to accomplish your primary activities, and sources for critical inputs to make your products and services. But even more important, you will begin to get a sense of what sets you apart from your competitors, if anything. You'll want to pay particular attention to technology development, because this support activity can provide important clues to your core competency, the topic of our next workshop.

Firm infrastructure. This support activity involves all the various general management functions you require to get the job done, including finance, accounting, information technology, legal, and other control systems to keep track of who is responsible for what in your company. Here, picture an organizational chart with various titles and arrows to indicate who's reporting to whom. But firm infrastructure goes beyond just the static organizational structure, to address the company's culture. What is the day-to-day atmosphere in the firm? Some company cultures are fast paced and aggressive, whereas others are more relaxed. Some firms will have more of a hierarchy, with clear delineations of responsibilities, whereas others will give their employees freer rein. Indeed, often company culture will depend on the industry it participates in. For example, the corporate culture at Walmart is all about being frugal and finding ways to cut costs from the company's operating structure while giving the customers what they want.[2] You can bet you'll find nothing lavish at Walmart's headquarters in Bentonville, Arkansas. On the other hand, fashion design houses like Ralph Lauren and Burberry are all about identifying and even creating tomorrow's fashion trends, so the corporate culture is likely to be built around creativity, design, and glamour. The concept of firm infrastructure can even be applied to your lemonade stand. If there's just one person running the stand, then the company, in effect, is a sole proprietorship with a simple organizational chart. All the functions are performed by one individual: you! Alternatively, three or four individuals may decide to operate the venture, so then the firm infrastructure would specify who does what. In addition, the culture of your lemonade stand may be more laid back. Maybe customers will come along, maybe they won't. Your competitor's culture, however, may be more lively as employees pursue sales by aggressively attracting customer attention.

Human resources management. Whom do you want working for you? Where do you find these capable people? How should you incentivize them to join your company? How should you compensate them? How do you train them? These questions are all answered under human resources management. In any organization, the most significant asset will be your employees. Without them, you'll never execute on even the greatest strategy in the world. You can easily see why choosing the right people can help even your simple lemonade stand. You may need talented people who know how to create one-of-a kind lemonade recipes using your freshly squeezed, organic lemons. Indeed, the more unique and differentiated your product, the more justified the $2-per-cup price of your lemonade will be. To compensate your salespeople, you can pay them an hourly wage. Some of your workers might need some training in making lemonade or in customer service. To boost employee morale, especially on hot days, you may even offer your workers free lemonade (as long as they don't cut significantly into your profits!).

Technology development. As mentioned previously, technology development should prompt you to think about what makes your company unique in the competitive marketplace. First, however, let us define what is meant by technology development. Or rather, let's start with what technology development is *not*: the number of desktop computers in your office, the latest packaged accounting software, or whether your company has a Facebook or LinkedIn page. Indeed, technology development does not involve those activities that make you operationally effective (from Workshop 1, those industry best practices that put you on a par with your competitors). Instead, you need to zero in on resources, capabilities, processes, and experiences that can set you apart from other companies in your industry. Here, technology development encompasses your collective learning within the organization that provides you with activities unique to the way you go about your business. These activities can enable you to offer goods and services at lower price points than those of your competitors (cost leadership), to create products or services that are completely different from your competitors' (differentiation), or even both, as long as you avoid the pitfalls of getting stuck in the middle! What exactly constitutes resources, capabilities, processes, experiences, and so forth is covered in the next workshop, on core competencies. However, to give you an example using your lemonade stand, a technology development could be Grandma's Special Recipe, especially if it were considered a trade secret, which uses beet sugar instead of cane sugar. Another example could be sourcing a unique organic lemon inaccessible to your competition. In the case of your differentiated all-organic, freshly squeezed lemonade, these two forms of technology development can help set you apart in the marketplace.

Procurement. The last support activity, procurement, involves accessing those materials, components, supplies, equipment, and so forth, necessary to produce your goods and services. You want to ensure a steady supply of the inputs needed for your operation. In other words, can you continue to find, secure, purchase, and have delivered those inputs that will allow you to create value-added offerings that you can sell in the market? Or do you need to consider alternate suppliers? Procurement as a support activity differs from the inbound logistics in the primary activities because of its external orientation. With procurement, you are more concerned with finding the suppliers of the inputs and making sure they will provide you with what you need. When considering your inbound logistics activities, on the other hand, you have already secured all the necessary inputs and are preparing for the actual production of your goods and services. Returning to your lemonade stand, your procurement activity involves finding suppliers of the aforementioned beet sugar or the organic lemons should you decide to purchase them from third parties.

Generic Strategies and the Value Chain

In an effort to describe the various primary and support activities of the value chain, we used a lemonade stand offering $2 freshly squeezed, organic lemonade. Its generic strategy is differentiation. You'll recall from the introduction to this workshop that your profit margin is dictated by how you arrange and perform the various activities in your value chain. In the case of your high-end lemonade stand, your inputs are more expensive (e.g., organic lemons, beet sugar, juicer). In addition, you have to complete a few extra steps to make fresh-squeezed lemonade: squeezing the lemons, getting the lemon-sugar ratio right, and so forth. However, while you have to contend with more expensive inputs as well as the added effort required to make freshly squeezed lemonade, you are hopeful that your product is unique and high quality enough that you can pass those costs on to the consumer in the form of a $2 price tag.

But what if you were to switch to a lemonade stand that competes on cost? That is, what if you offered lemonade using powdered lemonade mix, pricing the product at, say, 50 cents a cup? To compete effectively using an undifferentiated product (compared to your freshly squeezed, organic lemonade, it's relatively easier to go to the store, pick up powdered lemonade, and begin selling lemonade), you would try to undercut your competitors by pricing your lemonade as low as possible. All else being equal (e.g., price, customer service), consumers will choose the cheaper option. To understand how to compete effectively as a cost leader, you need to revisit all of the activities in your value chain to see where you can cut out unnecessary costs. Furthermore, you want to find ways to streamline your operation, especially since what you stand to lose in terms of profit margin you want to try to make up in volume. Let's look at the most obvious modifications in your value chain activities when switching to a cost leadership generic strategy.

Primary Activities

Inbound logistics. You will replace organic lemons, sugar, and a juicer with the less expensive, all-in-one powdered lemonade mix.

Operations. Your operation of making lemonade with powdered mix will be much less time-consuming and complicated. Instead of squeezing lemons, adding the right amount of sugar, and so forth, all you have to do is add water. This means that you can make—and try to sell!—much more lemonade in a shorter period of time.

Outbound logistics. Lemonade based on a powdered mix spoils less quickly than freshly squeezed, so you can cut out the expense of the curbside fridge.

Marketing and sales. While your marketing efforts using signage will be similar to those you used for the $2 organic lemonade, your message will be very different. Instead of highlighting your differentiated product, you will aggressively promote your low price of 50 cents per cup of lemonade. You may even advertise a group discount: buy five cups of lemonade, get the sixth free of charge! This approach will allow you to achieve the higher sales volume needed to make up for the thinner profit margin you realize on the cheaper product.

Service. How do you differentiate an undifferentiated product? If everyone in the neighborhood is selling the same powdered lemonade at 50 cents, how can you try to make your stand stick out? For starters, you should offer exceptional customer service. Low-cost competitors like online shoe retailer Zappos (now part of Amazon) and Southwest Airlines have perfected the art of providing exceptional, and even humorous, customer service. Another inexpensive way to distinguish your lemonade stand from the competition is to offer value-added services. For every cup sold, you may decide to donate five minutes of your time to community service. Finally, you can even collaborate with other local businesses to offer preferred vendor relations: buy my lemonade and receive a rebate on lawn-mowing services. This collaboration won't cost you anything, but it might provide additional incentive for your customers to buy product from you.

Support Activities

Firm infrastructure. Because your priority will be to sell your cheap lemonade in volume, you will have a relatively flat organizational infrastructure: one person cranking out lemonade with the rest selling, selling, selling. Indeed, the culture of your company will reflect this need to push product.

Human resource management. You may recall that the salespeople working for your freshly squeezed lemonade stand received an hourly wage. As you switch to competing on low prices, you may need to change the compensation structure for your sales team to a commission-based wage. This way, the more they sell (again, you want to sell in volume), the more they make. If they don't sell the lemonade, you don't have to compensate them.

Technology development. Can you think of ways to cut down significantly on the time it takes to make lemonade, since you're trying to sell cheap lemonade in large quantities? Indeed, if your competitors are slower than you, they'll be at a disadvantage, because after all, time is money. Maybe you know of this trick to speed up making lemonade with powdered mix: use hot water. If you just add cold water to powdered mix, it will take a long time for the powder to dissolve. You'll be stirring the pitcher for what seems an eternity. *But* using just a little bit of hot water at the outset instantly dissolves the powdered mix. Once it's dissolved, you can add cold water and ice, and you're off and running. This trick may be enough to give you a speed advantage over your competitors . . . at least until they find out about it.

Procurement. Compared to finding and securing access to beet sugar and organic lemons, your procurement activities with regard to powdered mix will be much more straightforward. Any grocery store will have a mix on its shelves, and you may even find it in bulk (economies of scale!) at Costco.

How you can use the value chain to tailor your activities to your company's particular strategy should be clear to you now. The lemonade stand example is a bit simplistic, but the concept of breaking down a business's activities to determine where and how value is created cuts across companies of any size. That said, let's stick with beverages and examine the value chain activities of a company with $30 million in annual sales, Reed's Inc. You'll see that the frameworks are just as effective.

Strategy in Action: Reed's World of Ginger

Anyone like ginger beer? If so, you may be familiar with Reed's, the company known for its ginger-flavored products, including its award-winning, nonalcoholic ginger brews, ginger teas, candies and chews, and even ice cream. Started in 1989 by Chris Reed, the company today sells its products in natural and organic grocery stores, such as Whole Foods Market, gourmet cafes, online (Amazon.com), and even drugstores. As a point of reference, a four-pack of 12-ounce Reed's Ginger Brew retails for about $7.

In relation to Coca-Cola and Pepsi, Reed's is a teeny-tiny company. So how does Reed's successfully go up against these Goliaths? By doing a value chain analysis of Reed's, you will gain important insights into the company's operations and how it delivers unique and targeted value to its customers.

However, before jumping into the value chain analysis, let's let the folks at Reed's tell you, in their own words, what they're all about. This statement is right off their Web page:[3]

> REED'S, Inc. is making extraordinary beverages and confections using very old-fashioned, natural methods and wholesome, fresh ingredients. We are a growing family of passionate entrepreneurs who have developed food and drink, which in our opinion exceed any products within their categories in taste, quality and imagination, as we are certain you noticed by now!

Reed's love for ginger has expanded to creating some delicious candies and even ice creams.

Recall that the starting point for any value chain analysis is the generic strategy. That is, depending on the generic strategy you select, the activities in the value chain need to be organized to fit that particular strategy. A company competing on (focused or broad-based) cost leadership emphasizes making its value chain activities as efficient and economical as possible. The value chain of a differentiator (focused or broad based), on the other hand, will reflect the value added to the product or service to command premium pricing from customers.

In terms of generic strategies, it would be extremely difficult for Reed's to compete based on price against Coca-Cola and Pepsi. These giants will always enjoy a clear advantage predicated on economies of scale and scope, thereby precluding Reed's taking up a cost leadership position. Although Reed's could try to occupy a focused cost leadership position as the lower-priced niche provider of ginger-related products, its emphasis on quality natural ingredients and sophisticated beverage brewing processes forces the company to pass on related costs of its operations to the end consumer in the form of a higher price: hence the $7 per four-pack of Reed's 12-ounce bottles.

This leaves only the differentiator or focused differentiator generic strategies for Reed's. An example of a differentiator in the U.S. carbonated soft drink market is Monster Beverage Corporation, the company behind Monster energy drinks, Hansen's Naturals, Blue Sky, and Peace Iced Tea. With over $2 billion in annual sales, Monster Beverage Corporation offers a wide range of premium-priced natural and specialty beverages. With its relatively limited lineup of beverages, its focus on ginger, its annual revenues of $30 million, and its premium-priced products, it quickly becomes apparent that Reed's firmly occupies a focused differentiator position.

Figure 6.2 presents Reed's value chain, highlighting those specific activities that allow the company to follow through on its generic strategy as a focused differentiator.

Primary activities. We begin on the left-hand side, where Reed's inbound logistics involve the preparation of its natural ingredients and other inputs to produce the finished goods. Its operations consist of developing and producing unique consumable products (e.g., brews, ice cream, candies), using ginger as the core ingredient for the majority of these products. In addition, Reed's flagship products, the ginger-based beverages, are manufactured using a proprietary brewing process that the company deems a

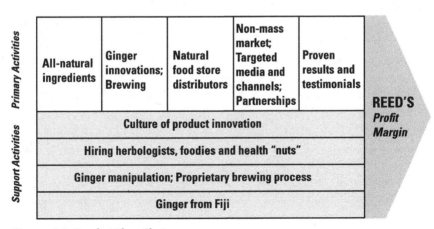

Figure 6.2. Reed's Value Chain

trade secret.[4] Moving on to outbound logistics, Reed's relies on a network of food service delivery companies such as United Natural Foods to distribute its products to natural and specialty food stores across the nation. Given its niche products, Reed's focuses its marketing and sales on targeted media and channels, using its highly trained sales force to work with distribution partners that place its products on grocery shelves. Based on the company's statements that ginger consumption delivers a multitude of health benefits, its service component extends beyond the usual product warranties to include research and testimonials to support and validate those particular health claims.

Support activities. Beginning in 1987, when Chris Reed began tinkering with brewing processes for sodas, Reed's has been a small but nimble competitor whose core activity is product innovation.[5] For Reed's to stay ahead of the pack, its culture of product innovation needs to permeate its firm infrastructure. A critical component is its human resource management of hiring, training, and retaining employees who can come up with the next generation of ginger-based products. These include herbologists, foodies, and even health "nuts" who embrace and promote the health benefits of Reed's products. Two specific aspects of Reed's technology development help the company create unique, premium products. First is its deep knowledge of, experience in, and expertise in manipulating (i.e., innovating) ginger into a variety of consumable products. Second is the brewing process the company has perfected over decades. Finally, Reed's experiences some exposure in its procurement because it sources its crystallized ginger for its chews from Fiji.[6] That's a long way to go to get a key ingredient. Furthermore, should the supplier in Fiji or the country itself become destabilized for some reason, the company's operation would experience a serious disruption until it could secure another source of crystallized ginger.

This value chain analysis for Reed's provides you with powerful operational insights into what the company does, and needs to continue doing, to successfully sell its premium products to a niche customer segment. The analysis also draws your attention to what, if anything, makes Reed's different or unique. Having highlighted "ginger innovation" and "proprietary brewing process" multiple times throughout our analysis, you probably now have a strong sense of Reed's core resources and capabilities.

In late 2009, Reed's purchased Sonoma Sparkler, a producer of sparkling apple, pear, lemonade, peach, orange, and raspberry juices.[7] Put your strategist hat on. If strategy involves trade-offs between what to do and what not to do, where do you envision this acquisition fitting into Reed's core resources and capabilities? If you're not entirely sure, follow us into the next workshop, on core competencies.

Workshop Takeaway

The value chain moves the strategic analysis from your industry and its related players inside your company. By dissecting your operations into primary activities and support activities, you can quickly get a clearer picture of where you can add value to your products and services. Your value chain should reflect your generic strategy. If you compete on cost, streamline your value chain for maximum efficiency; if you compete on differentiation, do something different or unique in your value chain that is reflected in the end product or service and allows you to charge a premium. The firmer your grasp of your company's value chain, the smoother your operations, the better your understanding of what makes you different in the marketplace, and the stronger your competitive footing.

The Core Competency: What's Your Secret Sauce?

In the first workshop, we likened the process of building a strategy to that of making a sandwich. Start with the bread (operational effectiveness); add your fillings of positioning, trade-off, and fit; and top it all off with the "secret sauce" of your unique activities. Having explored ways to strategically evaluate external competitive dynamics, as well as internal configurations that can enhance the value of your operation, you now need to ask yourself one of the most important questions in strategy: What, if anything, is my secret sauce? That is, what exactly makes you stick out from your competitors? What makes you different? Indeed, the entire point of having a strategy is to distinguish your company from all the others in the marketplace. If you are unable to do so, it would be pretty difficult for you to convince customers to buy your products or services rather than those of your competitors.

Our first goal in this workshop is to help you become familiar and conversant with the notion of core competencies.[1] We begin by defining what, exactly, constitutes a company's core competency. In our combined experience as strategists, one of the greatest challenges we come across when doing strategy workshops is getting managers and entrepreneurs to conceptualize their company in terms of its core competencies. You'll see shortly that the idea involves a radical shift in traditional thinking. You must move beyond understanding your company in terms of the products or services it sells and begin to recognize it for its resources, capabilities, and promises made to the consumer. Our second goal is to help you identify if in fact your company *has* a core competency. If so, how strong is it? Which parts of the company are aligned with the core competency? Which ones aren't? How can you go about boosting the company's core competency to provide you with a competitive advantage? Hang in there with us through the first part. How we define and conceive of a core competency may come across as a bit, well, esoteric. However, the exercises and examples at the end of the workshop should help crystallize your understanding of this concept.

Core Competencies Defined

Name the most direct competitors to the following consumer product brands:

Coca-Cola   McDonald's   Colgate

Your answers are Pepsi, Burger King, and Crest, right? But let's pause to ask what you pictured in your mind's eye when you thought of the answers: Was it the actual product? For Coca-Cola, did you conjure up a can or bottle of soda? Did a Big Mac pop into your head for McDonald's? And what about Colgate? Did you see yourself in the oral hygiene aisle at your local grocery store, staring at dozens of boxes containing toothpaste? If so, you are among the majority of people, including seasoned managers and entrepreneurs, who view a marketplace in terms of a company's, and its competitors', end products.

Here's the problem with this. Thinking only in terms of the products and services that a company feeds into the competitive environment may not only be extremely limiting, but may also lead you down the wrong path for your future endeavors. Indeed, if Coca-Cola and Pepsi had restricted themselves to trying to win the battle over their flagship products of carbonated sugar water, both of them would have missed out on some of the fastest-growing beverage categories over the past two decades: water, energy drinks, and fruit juices.[2]

Stripping an organization down to its core competency is a way to conceptualize it in terms of its assets, capabilities, organizational process, and firm attributes. A core competency also reaches into the knowledge, proficiencies, experiences, and expertise residing within the organization and its external network. It answers soul-searching questions about an organization's very existence: What do we, as an organization, know how to do? How do we know it? That is, how did we come to learn it? In turn, how do we apply this knowledge? What are the solutions we provide *based on* this combination of knowledge, experience, and expertise? What are the proficiencies, resources and capabilities, and even creative processes, required of us to provide those solutions? And last, how do we deliver on the promise made to the marketplace, to the customer? Notice that we did not mention the word *product* at any point.

When engaging in this line of questioning, your goal as a strategist is to look for the common thread that ties together all the various activities in your company. You're searching for the glue that binds together the existing businesses and operations. Just as important, your probing should begin to clarify your strategic intent, or where you are aiming your company's future efforts. Can your core competency offer the necessary springboard to tomorrow's opportunities? That is, in addition to allowing you to deliver value to your current customer base, is the core competency capable of tapping into additional markets? Do the company's brand and reputation convey your core competency to both present and future customers? Finally, does the core competency communicate to customers, suppliers, and even competitors what makes you different and unique, without you having to explicitly state it?

The Core Competency Tree

At this point, your brain is probably snapping, crackling, and popping! You may be saying to yourself, "easier said than done!" Let us introduce you to a handy tool that will simplify your quest to identify your company's core competency: the core competency tree. Figure 7.1 shows the tree and the four levels that make up its strategic architecture.

We begin at the top of the tree, with the end products that represent the products and services—the fruits, if you will—borne by the company. The next level consists of business units, or the branches in the tree. It is important to note here that these do not consist of functional business units such as marketing, accounting, and production. Rather, think of business units

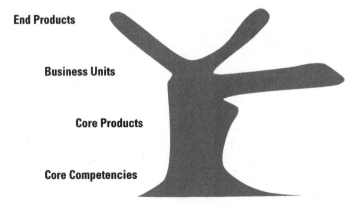

End Products

Business Units

Core Products

Core Competencies

Figure 7.1. The Core Competency Tree

as either the company's product/service categories *or* its customer-centric segments. So for the former, a company may have multiple products that can be lumped into groups. For Coca-Cola, for example, these groups may consist of carbonated and noncarbonated beverages. The latter classification, on the other hand, may reflect demographic and psychographic categories. Nike, for example, breaks its business units into consumers' interests: running, swimming, soccer, and so forth. The purpose in using the product/service grouping or customer-centric classifications for business units is to get you thinking about the common thread connecting the company's various activities to its demand-driven marketplace. Moving another level down, we reach the core products (or services). Representing the trunk of our core competency tree, core products make up the components, subassemblies, and so forth that underlie all of the end products. That is, although the end products may be aimed at different end markets/customers, they all have these core products in common. This applies to core services as well, where all the end services have a shared method, system, routine, or practice.

Here comes the difficult part: making the leap from core *products* to core *competencies*. Again, this requires you to think in terms not of products, but of the underlying capabilities, resources, processes, expertise, knowledge base, and so forth, that make those core products and, by extension, end products possible. In making that leap, you can get to the roots of your company's strategic architecture and, by extension, your competitive raison d'être.

When conducting this type of analysis to identify your company's core competency, start with the end products and work your way down the tree, sketching out the various parts of your strategic architecture. As you home in on the core competency, you need to continually ask yourself some hard questions:

- Is my company's core competency truly superior?
- How long can my company remain competitive if I don't protect this core competency?
- Can I leverage my company's core competency into other end markets, and if so, to what extent?
- Does the company's core competency clarify where I should allocate resources?
- Does my company's core competency make clear which competitive battles I should fight and which ones I should forego?
- Can my existing and future customers distinguish my company's core competency? What about my suppliers, resellers, and even competitors?
- Can I capture and articulate my company's core competency in a few short sentences?

It's important to keep in mind that this exercise involves an iterative process. That is, you have to loop back to the top of the tree a few times to probe deeper into various parts of it. You may find that certain core products, business units, or end products do not fit the common thread of your core competency. Indeed, these irrelevant and often isolated parts of your strategic architecture should draw your attention: Is this part of the business worth keeping? Does it provide for any competitive advantage? Can it be brought into alignment with the core competency, or should it be eliminated?

The Core Competency Test

With an accurate depiction of your company's strategic architecture through the core competency tree and having identified what you believe to be your company's core competency, you want to administer the core competency test, in the process asking how well the competency passes the test.

The core competency test consists of three powerful questions that attempt to capture the essence of your company's strategic uniqueness and long-term competitive advantage:

Question 1:   Does my company's core competency provide access to a wide variety of end markets?
We previously indicated that a company's core competency needs to serve as a springboard to future end markets. That is, it should provide you with the opportunity to enter other end markets that you currently are not serving, but may well want to at some later point. You may want to consider other end markets for the simple reason of expanding your business and accessing new revenue streams for continued growth. However, a second reason is that the end market your company currently serves can become destabilized or even irrelevant, forcing you to seek other end markets in an effort to remain competitive or even viable. Your company's core competency represents the pathway to those additional end markets.

Question 2:   Does my company's core competency contribute to the perceived customer benefits of end products/services?
Your company's core competency should convey to current and future customers the promise you make to the marketplace and how you go about delivering on that promise. Though your customers may not be able to explicitly express your company's core competency, they recognize what the company and its brands stand for. In this way, the core competency signals the value the company delivers to its customers through the end products or services. By extension, your company also inspires customers to reach for its products and services rather than those of competitors.

Question 3:   Is my company's core competency difficult to imitate or replace?
A core competency should be able to keep competitors at bay, at least for some time. If your rivals can quickly copy your company's core competency, thereby erasing what distinguishes your products and services in the marketplace, then your days are likely to be numbered. Similarly, your company's core competency can be replaced by the resources and capabilities of direct and even indirect competitors who will undermine your promise of value to current and future customers. It is therefore crucial that the core competency afford competitive protection, at least for some time, and that those protective barriers continue to be nurtured.

There are a few additional things to keep in mind when administering the core competency test. First, a company can, and often does, have more than one core competency. That said, we have found that the exercise to identify core competencies often leads people to build extensive lists without paying heed to what, exactly, is truly unique or superior about a company. A company will only have a few competencies that make it stick out from its competitors. Second, core competencies should be neither too generic nor too narrow. "Quality" is not a core competency, especially because it's a very subjective term; what encompasses quality to one person can signify something completely different to another. Distilling core competencies down to their essence is therefore vital. That said, keep in mind that core competencies that are too narrow may not provide the necessary springboard to future end markets. Third, multiple core competencies in a company often strengthen one another. As in our discussion of the concept of fit in Workshop 1, there is often a synergistic and reinforcing effect to core competencies. This means that focusing on one core competency without paying heed to the others can weaken the company's overall competitive standing. To help illustrate the usefulness of conceptualizing core competencies and the technique to identify them, let's turn to the automotive world.

Honda's Core Competency

Question: Why do Honda cars have some of the highest resale values in the automotive industry? Is it because of their styling? Or is it because drivers associate the brand with a certain lifestyle, as is the case with Subaru? If your answer is "Because they run forever!" you're not only touching on Honda's promise to the market, you're also tapping directly into the company's core competency. Figure 7.2 depicts and fully captures Honda's core competency.

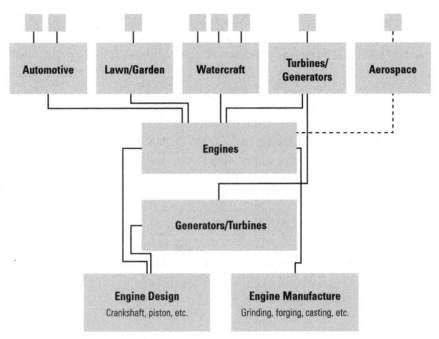

Figure 7.2. Honda's Core Competency Tree

Let's begin by listing some of the end products that Honda sells in the marketplace. The most obvious is Honda's car brands: Honda Pilot, Honda Accord, and Honda Civic. But Honda is so much more than just a car company. In addition to manufacturing automobiles, Honda also makes and sells motorcycles and scooters; all-terrain vehicles (ATVs); lawn mowers; snowblowers; outboard motors for boats; and even stand-alone engines for pressure washers, industrial equipment, and agricultural applications. You will note some of these end products in the core competency. For business units, you can place all of these products into their respective product categories: automotive for all the cars, motorcycles, scooters, and ATVs; landscaping for the lawn mowers, snowblowers, tillers, and trimmers; marine for the boating products; and turbines and generators for the stand-alone engines. You could also classify Honda's products into two broad categories, consumer and commercial, but you would lose quite a bit of detail in the core competency tree, thereby running the risk of not discovering the common thread that binds all the products.

Once you have identified the appropriate business units, you can move to the next level by asking: What are the core products that underlie all the end products? That is, what are the common components or subcomponents that you can find in all of the end products? By now, you're probably beginning to see an emerging picture: engines. Whether you're looking at a Honda Odyssey minivan, the HRX21 series of lawn mowers, or the 105-horsepower jet outboard motor, at the core you will find a Honda engine, turbine, or generator. To make the leap to Honda's core competency, you now need to move away from visualizing "products" and sum up what it is that Honda, as an organization, does best. In other words, what are its resources and capabilities? What is Honda's knowledge base? What do the people who work at Honda really know how to do, probably better than anyone else out there? It may seem obvious now that we've worked systematically down our core competency tree: engine design, manufacturing, and assembly. Honda is unparalleled in the design of crankshafts, cylinders, pistons, and so forth. And it is expert in grinding, forging, casting, machining, and assembling all those engine parts into a whole. No wonder Honda keeps extremely tight controls on its manufacturing plants throughout the world. Whereas other automotive OEMs (original equipment manufacturers, or brands) constantly shop around for cost-effective third-party manufacturers, Honda recognizes the importance of protecting its proficiency and expertise in engine design and manufacturing. Without that, it's just another car company without a distinguishing and unique characteristic that makes it stick out in a crowded marketplace. And without its core competency, Honda is incapable of delivering its promise to the automotive consumer of cars that are durable and reliable—cars that seemingly run forever.

In the early 2000s, conglomerate General Electric approached Honda with a unique proposition: Would Honda consider partnering with GE to develop engines for use in business jets? While GE has had a long history in the aerospace business, it wanted to access Honda's core competency to design and make durable and, very important, reliable engines for use in private jet airplanes. In 2004 the two companies entered into a joint venture, GE Honda Aero Engines, which has resulted in the successful production of the GE Honda HF120, a small turbofan engine.[3]

The Honda example demonstrates that the company has been able to successfully use its core competency as a springboard to a variety of end markets (automotive, marine, aerospace, etc.). And as consumers and even GE seem to recognize, the Honda brand effectively and powerfully conveys and delivers a clear and distinctive promise to the marketplace. In terms of passing the final core competency test, to understand to what extent Honda's core competency is difficult to imitate or replace, picture this scenario: You're sitting in a window seat on a plane. Seconds before takeoff, you take your eyes off your in-flight magazine, glance out the window, and focus on the jet engine under the wing of the plane. You can just make out the name of the jet engine manufacturer. It reads Buick. Enjoy your flight!

Strategy in Action: The Promise Behind the Brand

To further hone your thinking about core competencies, take a moment to think through the well-known brands and try to determine what, exactly, they say about the company behind them; that is, what is the implicit promise to the consumer? And by extension, what unique resources and capabilities does the company rely on to deliver on that promise, if any? You may want to sketch out a core competency tree, starting at the top with a sampling of end products and working your way down until you get to the core competency.

- Nike
- McDonald's
- Walmart
- Gerber
- Disney
- Dell
- Volvo
- Apple

Ready?

Nike. Nike wants you to "just do it." That is, it wants its customers to get off the couch and go for a run, shoot some hoops, and hit the fairway. To help them "do it," Nike offers consumers the latest designs in sports apparel and equipment, from soccer balls to tennis shoes to football helmets. So, Nike's sports apparel and equipment design know-how is one core competency. But that's not all. To inspire and motivate those of us who are less athletically inclined, Nike locks in star athletes and engages them in highly memorable television commercials and other marketing campaigns. In fact *The Onion*, a satirical news source, picked up on Nike's core competency a few years ago when it released the following mock announcement: Nike would cease manufacturing athletic shoes and other sports-related merchandise so as to devote itself fully to the creation of state-of-the-art advertisements and remain the leader in incredibly cool television commercials.[4]

McDonald's. How does McDonald's keep hold of its reign in fast food? Just in the burger category alone, there are seemingly endless competitors: Burger King, Wendy's, Sonic, Jack in the Box, Arby's, Hardees, White Castle . . . the list goes on. So why then does McDonald's continue to dominate? Is it because its burgers taste better than any others? Though some people may be quick to make that claim, many have probably sunk their teeth into far better burgers. But McDonald's does have two highly distinguishable features to its business: convenience and standardization. With respect to convenience, McDonald's is indeed everywhere. Domestically, you will find its restaurants in urban, suburban, and rural communities, as well as the airports that take you from one community to another. And McDonald's has successfully expanded to over 118 countries, currently clocking in at over 34,000 store locations worldwide.[5] Indeed, 75 McDonald's burgers are sold every second of every day . . . there go another 150![6] McDonald's other core competency is standardization. That is, you can order a Big Mac, whether in Venice, California, or Venice, Italy, and be assured that it will taste the same. Sure, there might be some customization in local markets (no beef patties in India!), but for the most part, the fare will taste similar everywhere. McDonald's can achieve this standardization largely because of its sophisticated supply chain, which controls all aspects of sourcing, distribution, preparation, cooking, and delivery of its food items. It is little wonder then that U.S. backpackers abroad, seeking a taste of home, sooner or later head to the Golden Arches.

Walmart. We have touched on Walmart in previous workshops, alluding to some of its core competencies. One reason Walmart is able to efficiently and effectively sell such an enormous amount of goods is its logistics infrastructure. Using a sophisticated information technology system rivaling that of the Pentagon, Walmart has clear visibility of the products that fly off its store shelves.[7] This information allows Walmart to dictate to its thousands of vendors the exact specifications (quantities, sizes, colors, etc.) of the products it wants to stock in each and every store. But Walmart has another related core competency: its size. A company's size can be a liability, but in the case of Walmart, it is a core competency. Why? First, its volume sales have been earned over time, beating out competitors such as Target, Kohl's, and other retail chains. And second, for Walmart, the sheer magnitude of stuff bought and sold allows it to squeeze its suppliers for extensive price concessions.

Gerber. Gerber today is a subsidiary of Swiss food giant Nestlé. That said, even as a division of a larger company, Gerber relies on its core competency to maintain its competitive advantage in an increasingly crowded marketplace. What exactly is that core competency? First, let's review some of the products under the Gerber umbrella: baby food, pacifiers, baby bottles, toys, onesies, and receiving blankets. Indeed, Gerber's products span from pregnancy through toddler and beyond. In addition to all these care products, Gerber also sells investment services through Gerber Life Insurance Company, including term and whole-life insurance, college plans, and accident protection plans. Looking at all these products and services, what is Gerber's promise to the market? Simply put, peace of mind for parents. By providing parents with the products and services they need to feed, clothe, clean, and protect their children, Gerber helps alleviate some of the stress, anxiety, and confusion of parenting. For

Gerber to continue to deliver on this promise, it must adhere to strict quality control standards across all of its products and services. By gaining the trust of doctors and forging partnerships with clinics and hospitals, Gerber can make sure to be the first brand parents encounter when they know they're expecting!

Disney. Yes, Disney equals entertainment. But there's more. After all, any movie production company, music label, or video game developed falls into the category of entertainment. With Disney, we can add *family* entertainment. And here's the other layer: character-driven merchandising. Disney knows how to conceive of movie characters (Mickey Mouse, Cinderella, Buzz Lightyear, etc.) that translate into a slew of other products and services: Mickey Mouse T-shirts, Cinderella backpacks, Buzz Lightyear toys, and amusement park rides. Disney also owns ESPN, the sports cable network, which has been highly profitable for the company. That said, in dire times, would Disney be more likely to sell off ESPN or its family entertainment–related properties? Let's put this another way: Who has more staying power, Snow White or Nick Faldo? If you're not familiar with the latter name, point made. On another note, in 2009 Disney acquired Marvel Comics, the company behind comic book characters such as Spiderman, Iron Man, and the Incredible Hulk, among many others.[8] While Marvel fits perfectly alongside Disney's core competency of character-driven merchandising, it is less aligned with the family entertainment competency. The risk in this misalignment, as some have noted, is that Marvel Comics fans, who generally tend to be older and predominantly male, may not want to be affiliated with Disney's younger consumer base. Disney's top management is keenly aware of this, making sure to keep the two entities quite separated. You probably won't see Captain America rides in Disneyland, nor will Donald Duck join the Fantastic Four in any upcoming comics.

Dell. In a previous workshop, we identified Dell's generic strategy as "stuck in the middle," because it is getting squeezed by larger cost players such as Acer and HP on one side and Apple's differentiation on the other. Although Dell rose to prominence on a unique business model of direct-to-customer, built-to-order PCs, it now offers an insightful example of what happens to a company when its core competency is not difficult to imitate or replace. As other PC manufacturers quickly adopted this business model, it transformed into an industry best practice, thereby undermining Dell's competitive advantage and leaving it to rebuild its core competency elsewhere. Dell's search for a new core competency continues to this day.

Volvo. Did you say safety? Generally, most folks, when they think about Volvo cars, will probably say that Volvo makes some of the safest cars on the road. A few years ago, when Volvo introduced its racy coupe convertible, its ads made sure to mention—front and center—that this new model was both fun *and* safe. Although the car division of Volvo is today owned by Chinese car manufacturer Geely, its new parent continues to sell the car on its core competency of safety engineering.

Apple. Let's let the folks at Apple tell us themselves. This is straight from Apple's annual report:

The Company's business strategy leverages its unique ability to design and develop its own operating system, hardware, application software, and services to provide its customers new products and solutions with superior ease-of-use, seamless integration, and innovative industrial design. The Company is therefore uniquely positioned to offer superior and well-integrated digital lifestyle and productivity solutions.[9]

In short, Apple's core competency is digital lifestyle and productivity solutions based on ease of use, hardware and software integration, and industrial design.

Workshop Takeaway

When pared down to its essence, having a strategy means "sticking out" from your competitors. The core competency of a company allows it to leverage its unique set of resources, capabilities, skills, experiences, and human capital in an effort to achieve long-term competitive advantage. Identifying and building your core competency begins with thinking beyond your company in terms of products and services. Keep asking: What is my company's promise to my customers, and how do I go about delivering on that promise? The core competency tree is an effective visual tool to home in on your company's common thread and also helps to point out those activities that, strategically speaking, simply don't fit. Once you know which battles to fight and which to forego, you can begin to grow your company. We discuss your strategic approach to expansion in the next workshop.

Diversifications: Where Do You Go from Here—and How Do You Get There?

As mentioned throughout this book, the frameworks covered in the workshops are wholly integrative, working in unison to sharpen our strategic visions. Having identified the competitive dynamics in the external environment and delved into the strategic factors that can make our company "stick out," we are now in a position to ask questions about growth, expansion, and diversification. You might be thinking, "Growing my firm is my top priority—why are we talking about it only now?" Benjamin Hoff, best-selling author of *The Tao of Pooh*, succinctly captures our sentiments when it comes to the importance of strategic thinking before setting off on a growth path: "How can you get very far, if you don't know who you are? How can you do what you ought, if you don't know what you've got?"[1]

In this workshop, we'll acquaint you with the Product–Market Growth Matrix, a simple yet powerful framework devised by strategist Igor Ansoff.[2] This particular tool allows you to explore and recognize the risks relating to your expansionary efforts. You'll recall from our introduction that there are no right or wrong strategies, because the outcomes of your strategic decisions become apparent only after the fact. The best you can do, as a strategic thinker, is try to identify the risks inherent in the strategic choices you make. Before jumping into the Product–Market Growth Matrix, we illustrate the strategic link between a firm's core competency and its considerations for growth.

Beyond the Restaurant Business: McDonald's

Constantinos Markides, a strategy professor at the London School of Business, presented a particular scenario to a group of seasoned managers enrolled in an executive education program.[3] The scenario was simple: you're the CEO of McDonald's and faced with the following three expansion strategies:

1. McDonald's develops frozen foods, to be sold in grocery store chains.
2. McDonald's launches amusement parks, to compete against Six Flags, Disney, and others.
3. McDonald's offers photo processing services.

If you had to choose one, which would it be, and why? Take a moment to think through the various options.

At first glance, all these options may seem a bit off-base, especially considering McDonald's base business of selling burgers and fries through its restaurants. However, each of these expansion strategies draws to some extent from McDonald's core competencies. You'll recall from the previous workshop that we identified the company's core competencies as convenience and standardization. Let's take a look at the various options and how they connect to these competencies.

McDonald's develops frozen foods, to be sold in grocery store chains. You could probably envision McDonald's deciding to bag McDonald's-branded frozen fries and selling them through grocery outlets, including Walmart, Safeway, and others. This would certainly be convenient for consumers. Just as you can brew Starbucks coffee at home, you would now be able to heat up McDonald's fries in your kitchen. However, to what extent does this strategic initiative link up to McDonald's other core competency of standardization? As we noted previously, McDonald's achieves the standardization of its global fare based on its tight management of food sourcing, distribution, preparation, cooking, and delivery. But selling frozen fries in grocery stores would effectively hand over the cooking portion to the customer at home, causing McDonald's to lose control over the standardization of the end product as some customers undercook or overcook the fries. The risk with this expansion strategy is that it undermines the product consistency that McDonald's customers have come to expect from the company.

McDonald's launches amusement parks, to compete against Six Flags, Disney, and others. An expansion strategy involving amusement parks has a level of appeal. Like Disney, McDonald's already has a cast of characters that may entice kids, including Ronald McDonald, Grimace, the Hamburgler, and close on his heels, Officer Big Mac. These are just a few among a surprisingly large troupe. Furthermore, numerous retail outlets already have play structures called PlayPlaces, which afford parents a short respite from their kids. Yet though McDonald's core competencies may help it effectively manage some aspects of its amusement parks, they are not central to the resources and capabilities needed to be successful in this business. That is, its food-based convenience and standardization would take a backseat to the necessary skills of developing rides, creating a unique experience, and so forth. Without a doubt, both Disney and Six Flags have a leg up on McDonald's when it comes to amusement parks.

McDonald's offers photo processing service. This expansion strategy may certainly seem dated today, given the shift toward digital photography and in-home photo processing, if indeed those digital pictures get processed at all in this day and age! Nevertheless, stick with us on this strategic initiative. As you'll see shortly, there is merit to it.

Let's envision the following: photo-processing kiosks in McDonald's restaurants. A McDonald's customer who frequents the chain once or twice a week may want to take a few extra minutes to upload pictures from a thumb drive to print out hard copies of digital pictures. It's convenient, and the kiosks produce a consistent product. In that way, this initiative takes advantage of both McDonald's ubiquity as well as its standardization. You may well be saying to yourself: If that's the case, then why wouldn't McDonald's get into, say, the video rental business? Well, in effect, it did. Heard of Redbox, the video rental kiosks where you can rent a movie DVD for a $1 a day? McDonald's was the company that founded Redbox, launching the rental kiosks in 2003 in Las Vegas and Washington, D.C.[4] Six years later, it successfully sold Redbox to Coinstar for a nice return on its investment.

The Product–Market Growth Matrix

What the McDonald's exercise demonstrates is that a company's future strategy is predicated wholly on its core competency. You want to keep this in mind as you contemplate the following questions: Which business am I going to enter? How will I grow it? Expand it? Diversify it? And concurrently, which business am I going to forego or even exit? For clarity in answering these questions, refer to the Product–Market Growth Matrix in figure 8.1.

The two labels of our matrix are "Market" (e.g., customer segments, distribution channels, geographic) and "Product" (products and services). When contemplating your company's growth, the matrix indicates that you have four distinct options. First, you can continue to push your current lineup of products or services into your existing market, or the market where you are currently selling. Second, you can take your existing lineup of products and services and try to expand into new segments, geographic

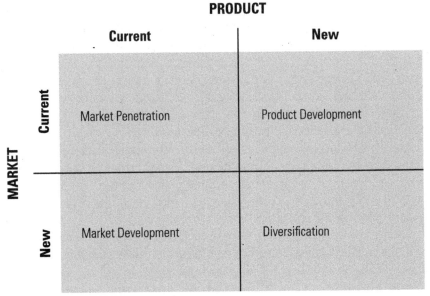

Figure 8.1. The Product–Market Growth Matrix

areas, and/or distribution channels. Third, you can develop new products and see if your existing customers have any interest in buying them. And last, you may come up with new products and services and simultaneously seek out new markets in which to sell them. As we detail below using McDonald's as an example for each initiative, every option carries with it its own level of risk.

Market Penetration

Market penetration: If you're engaged in market penetration, your main concern is selling more of your existing products and services in your current target market. In other words, you have already gained some initial traction in your base business, but are now looking to penetrate the market further (gain additional market share), either by acquiring new customers or by boosting purchases and use of your product or service by existing customers. This can be done through sales and marketing, advertising, promotion, and discounting (seasonal, coupons, etc.), as well as other customer acquisition and retention programs.

Market penetration risk: In most circumstances, market penetration, relative to the other quadrants, entails the lowest level of risk. Think about it. You have an established product or service and are selling it into a market that is willing to buy it. Your priority is simply to sell more of the product or service. One caveat: if you're in the business of selling buggy whips (or any other product that is experiencing diminishing demand), a path of continued market penetration will not help solve your strategic problems. In cases like these, as we have discussed regarding Dell's PC business, market penetration indeed becomes the riskiest Product–Market Growth initiative.

Market Penetration Example: McDonald's Relaunches Its Dollar Menu

Since 2002, McDonald's has periodically launched its popular Dollar Menu, consisting of $1 items, including its double cheeseburger, McChicken, fries, sundaes, and other items. The promotion, which McDonald's touts as "a tasty way to fill up for less," is meant to drive additional purchases from existing customers as well as steal away customers from fast-food competitors such as Burger King and Wendy's. In other words, the Dollar Menu allows McDonald's to generate additional fast-food market share (i.e., to further penetrate the market).

Market Development

Market development: When pursuing market development, you are intent on taking your current/existing product or service and expanding it into new markets. These new markets may involve a different customer segment (males to females, teens to adults, early technology adopters to late technology adopters, etc.), another geographic market (domestic to international, rural to urban/suburban, etc.), or entirely new distribution channels (wholesale to retail, offline to online, etc.).

Market development risk: Although you will be familiar with your current products and services, the new market, with which you are unfamiliar, raises the risk of an unknown variable: Will your product gain acceptance by the new customer segment? Will it translate in a different geographic market? Can it be sold and distributed effectively and efficiently in the distribution channel you're considering? Relative to market penetration, in most circumstances, market development involves a higher level of risk to your business.

Market Development Example: McDonald's Goes Abroad

McDonald's today serves its fast-food fare in more than 34,000 outlets in 118 countries, including Brunei and Cuba. Many of the meal products offered in these locations are the same you would expect to find in U.S. locations: Big Macs, Filet-O-Fish sandwiches, French fries, and so forth. In taking its existing products abroad, into new markets, McDonald's engaged in market development. The risks involved include, among others, understanding the consumer habits in a different country, setting effective promotional and pricing strategies, finding the right store locations, staffing, and training.

Product Development

Product development: The pursuit of product development is a reversal of market development. You're introducing new products and services to your existing customers. These new products and services don't have to be radically different; they can just involve new features, upgrades, add-ons, and so forth. Think Vista, Microsoft's operating system introduced in 2007. In effect, Vista was an upgrade to its previous operating system, Windows XP, geared toward its current individual, educational, and commercial customers.

Product development risk: With the introduction of Vista, Microsoft experienced firsthand the risks of product development. Customers and technology reviewers pummeled the software upgrade with heavy criticism because of its reconfigured features and components, its restricted software compatibility, and its slow and bulky performance.[5] Here, the risk was offering customers something new that, in the end, they didn't want or need. New Coke, anyone?

Product Development Example: McDonald's Introduces Gourmet Salads

In the mid-1980s, McDonald's added a selection of gourmet salads to its menu in an effort to appeal to the more health-conscious consumer. In providing existing customers with a healthy meal option, this initiative represented a product development. But wait: What about potential customers who previously didn't consider frequenting McDonald's for a healthy meal? In this latter case, McDonald's aimed to draw in new customers with a new product, which corresponds with a diversification strategy. And indeed, it was relatively riskier for McDonald's to create new customers with its gourmet salads than to give existing customers an option to switch their fries for leafy greens.

Diversification

Diversification: As just discussed, when launching new products or services into unfamiliar markets, you're pursuing a diversification strategy.

The basic idea behind diversification is that you may not want to have all your business eggs in one basket. As a strategy, diversification was quite popular in the 1960s and 1970s; for example, oil companies owned movie studios. However, the 1980s experienced a movement among publicly traded companies to narrow their scope of activities and focus their efforts and resources on competing successfully in a few businesses, or even just one.

Diversification risk: Because diversification involves two unknowns—the products/services and the customers segments/channels/geographic areas—this strategy involves a relatively higher level of risk than the other quadrants in the Product–Market Growth Matrix. In addition, although spreading business bets across sectors and industries may seem like a way to lower your risk exposure, managing disparate companies can be quite complicated. Even conglomerate companies like General Electric, which once produced everything from lightbulbs and toasters to CAT scan machines and freight train engines, are revamping their businesses to align with a common theme (yes, core competency!).

Diversification Example: McDonald's Enters India

Why is McDonald's foray into the Indian market an example of diversification and not market development? What's different about India? The answer is simple: India's predominant religion, Hinduism, forbids the killing and eating of cows. That's a hurdle when your chief product is beef burgers. To crack this market, McDonald's developed an entirely new menu consisting of largely vegetarian sandwiches, including the McVeggie and the McCurry Pan. That is, McDonald's expanded with two unknowns: a new product *and* a new market. Relative to the other international markets, where McDonald's could simply introduce its existing products, its expansion into India was indeed riskier.

We hope that we have been able to convey the real benefit of using the Product–Market Growth Matrix to explore and understand the risks underlying your growth initiatives. As our examples indicate, depending on how you view an expansionary strategy, it can involve either a higher or lower level of risk. In the case of McDonald's product launch of gourmet salads, the "lower-hanging fruit" for generating sales involves getting existing customers to opt for a healthy food choice rather than trying to convince new customers to consider McDonald's as a healthy fast-food outlet. For ease of reference, figure 8.2 shows the related levels of risk for each quadrant in the Product–Market Growth Matrix.

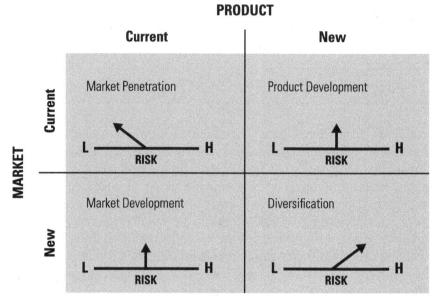

Figure 8.2. Risk Levels in the Product–Market Growth Matrix

Keep in mind that the risk of an initiative is determined by its related-ness to the company's core competencies, not its existing products and ser-vices. As McDonald's venture into DVD rentals demonstrates, although the end products may be quite different, a company can capitalize on certain technologies, processes, marketing know-how, and so forth, in its expan-sionary efforts. The key questions to keep asking yourself as you explore growth strategies follow:

- *Am I succeeding with my market penetration?* Since venturing from your core busi-ness (current product/service in current markets) increases the risks to your company, you want to make sure you are pursuing and successfully achieving market penetration. Additional market penetration is often the lower-hanging fruit, so your business can experience a low-risk growth boost from simply tweaking your sales and marketing efforts, seeking out alternate advertising media and promotional channels, trying different discounting initiatives, and launching customer acquisition and retention programs.
- *Is my expansion strategy proactive or reactive?* When pursuing a proactive expan-sion strategy, a company is mostly on solid footing with respect to its current product/service and current markets. That is, with the initial business established and the core competency providing for critical protective barriers from competi-tors, the company can venture into uncharted waters with the knowledge that it can always fall back on its core business. Reactive expansions, in contrast, involve struggling companies faced with thinning opportunities in their core markets. As

they lose ground to increased competition, more discriminating customers, or technological shifts, these companies are forced to take up market development, product development, or diversification. The risk of pursuing new products and services, new markets, or both is compounded by the risks of staying or having to retreat back to a core market with unfavorable growth prospects.

- *Which new sets of rivals will I encounter as I expand?* As you expand your product lines and grow your markets, your business is bound to bump up against new categories of competitors. Consider the following example. When Apple entered the smartphone market, launching its iPhone in 2007, it started competing with a whole new set of opponents, namely cell phone manufacturers. Whereas its original rivals included Microsoft, Dell, HP, and other players in the PC software and hardware business, Apple added companies such as Nokia, Motorola, and Blackberry to its competitive landscape. For Apple, this meant that it needed to learn new rules of engagement and strategically position itself with respect to the strengths and weaknesses of the established cell phone manufacturers.

By this point in *Mastering Strategy* you have been exposed to the most prevalent and popular strategy frameworks that can help you evaluate your industry's competitive dynamics, determine your company's competitive position within that industry, and map your growth initiatives based on your company's core competencies. We reiterate: these frameworks work in unison to provide strategic clarity about your competitive advantage. That said, the analysis is never complete. Rather, strategic thinking comprises a continuous, iterative loop. Take, for example, this last framework, the Product–Market Growth Matrix. Having determined which expansionary path to pursue, you will have to circle back to the external environment again to ask yourself: What is the *new* P-E-S-T-E-L faced by my company as I expand? Are there any industry changes I need to be aware of as I expand? What are the opportunities and threats in the *new* market I intend to enter? How do my strengths and weaknesses line up with those opportunities and threats? What do the five competitive forces of the new product and/or new market look like? That is, which competitive forces are bound to chip away at my overall profitability, and how can I position my company favorably to mitigate those forces? And yes, the next step will involve evaluating the new value system to see who is kicking whom and kissing whom. Alas, you can see that the work of a strategic thinker is never done.

Strategy in Action: Identity Crisis at Crocs

Crocs shoes . . . love 'em or hate 'em, that seems to be the general sentiment about these rubber clogs. Founded in 2002, Crocs quickly became not just a financial success, but also a cultural phenomenon. Celebrity Chef Mario Batali, actor/comedian Adam Sandler, and even the forty-seventh U.S. president, George W. Bush, have been spotted on more than one occasion sporting the (in)famous shoes. In less than a decade, Crocs rang up over $1 billion in annual sales.

But everything hasn't always gone well in the Land of Crocs. In 2008–2009, the company came dangerously close to bankruptcy, accumulating losses of close to $200 million. And its price per share fell from a high of $68 to just over $1. Since then, Crocs has been fighting an uphill battle, trying to find its footing (pun intended) in the shoe world. Numerous competitors, including the start-up Holey's and the juggernaut Walmart, have flooded the market with cheaper knockoffs. In addition, a few high-profile accidents, as well as its function-over-fashion branding, have resulted in a global consumer backlash. With diminishing product differentiation and brand loyalty, Crocs has its work cut out for it.

Stay with us as we give you a sense of how the strategy frameworks covered in the previous workshops can provide important insights into Crocs' strategic mishaps. You'll see that we question Crocs' very existence as a shoe designer and marketer and that a very different fate could have befallen this company, if only it had thought of itself and its competition in completely different ways. Let's go back to the spring of 2008.

On May 14, 2008, Crocs issued a press release introducing Citiesbyfoot.com, a Web-based travel guide to shops, boutiques, restaurants, bars, and other attractions in six U.S. cities. The purpose of Citiesbyfoot.com, according to Crocs' management, was to give Crocs customers "desirable walking destinations that exhibit entrepreneurial spirit, quality products and colorful thinking around the world."[6] Management stressed that Citiesbyfoot.com provided Crocs with an entry point in the burgeoning Web video market.

Your strategic instincts may be telling you that something is amiss with Crocs' launch of Citiesbyfoot.com. And yes, the Crocs' press release does open the door to a set of questions: Does CitiesByFoot.com align with what Crocs does best? How risky is it for Crocs to get into the burgeoning Web video market? Finally, should Crocs have put its efforts elsewhere?

As we answer these questions using our toolkit of strategy frameworks, we will begin to see that Crocs' product launch of CitiesByFoot.com is not the root cause of the company's woes, but rather a symptom of a much larger problem concerning its identity crisis. Figure 8.3 is a core competency tree for Crocs at the time of its foray into the travel guide business.

Crocs' end products include various models of rubber clogs, leather shoes, Jibbitz shoe charms, accessories such as cell phone holders, knee-pads, handbags, hats, shirts . . . and CitiesByFoot.com.

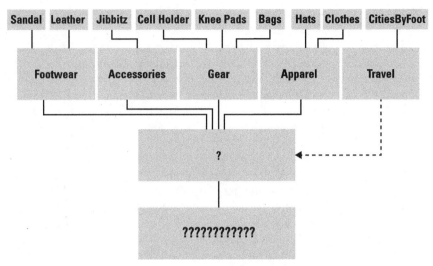

Figure 8.3. Crocs' Current Core Competency Tree

In reviewing these end products, we need to ask: What are the core products that underlie all the end products? And what are the company's resources, capabilities, skills, and so forth, that can provide it a competitive advantage? Is there a common thread holding together this core competency tree? If you're struggling to identify that common thread, you're not alone. Although many of the end products fall under the general category of "apparel," whittling these end products down to their core products and, by extension, core competencies poses a significant challenge. After all, what do cotton T-shirts, CitiesByFoot.com, and rubber clogs have in common?

Going back to the resources, capabilities, and skills that gave Crocs its initial competitive advantage when it launched in 2002 can help us understand where the company got off track.[7] The sources of Crocs' early success were the following:

A low-cost, "funky" product design. Besides pioneering a radical and colorful shoe design in its rubber clogs, Crocs' innovation also involved a relatively low-cost production process. Unlike conventional shoes that require heavy manual labor involvement, Crocs relied on injection-molding machines. At a push of a button, Crocs could literally crank out huge volumes of its clogs.

Grassroots marketing campaigns. Crocs' early promotional channels were largely based on word of mouth. For starters, Crocs initially targeted niche segment customers for whom Crocs made sense: gardeners, boaters, and nurses. Indeed, getting celebrities such as chef Mario Batali to wear Crocs helped to make them popular and instantly recognizable. With time, noncustomers started seeing customers wearing Crocs in the street and asked them: "What are those?!" And more important, "Where can I get a pair?"

Focus on small, independent retailers. In contrast to big-box stores like Walmart and Target, smaller independent retailers were much more willing to put Crocs' new but unproven clogs in their window displays. To help these retailers sell product, Crocs provided simple yet effective rotating display racks: Customers could scan for a color and shoe size by themselves without assistance from a store clerk. This customer convenience helped Crocs' clogs fly off the shelves— or, rather, racks.

Highly flexible global supply chain. Crocs' management took cues from other businesses, especially those in the PC and electronics industries, to streamline its supply chain and make it highly responsive to growing product demand. By relying on multiple contract manufacturers largely in China, Crocs was prepared to rapidly adjust its production volume to meet market demand in the United States and, eventually, abroad.

Innovation using Croslite. Crocs' rubber clogs are produced using a one-of-a-kind material called Croslite, its proprietary and patented closed-cell foam resin. Pioneered by a company called Foam Creations, Croslite has a unique set of characteristics: it is lightweight, antimicrobial, odor-resistant, and nonmarking (i.e., it won't leave surface marks).

But to what extent do these resources, capabilities, and skills still hold up today? If we take into consideration Crocs' competitive dynamics arising from new rivals, consumer backlash, and big-box retailers, we quickly find that its protective barriers and its uniqueness have eroded over time:

A low-cost, "funky" product design. Crocs' success with its rubber clogs has invited numerous competitor products, many of which are sold at a much lower price. There is even a rampant market for Crocs counterfeits.

Grassroots marketing campaigns. Though its grassroots marketing campaign helped the company initially gain popularity, today Crocs is focused largely on maintaining and growing market share through new shoe and apparel introductions.

Focus on small, independent retailers. Whereas smaller retailers comprised Crocs' initial sales channels, big-box retailers such as Target, Kohl's, and niche players including Famous Footwear now push volumes of its products. And as we have mentioned in the Walmart example, these volume retailers can, and do, exert significant pricing pressure on Crocs.

Highly flexible global supply chain. Take another quick look at some of the end products in the core competency tree. Did you notice the leather shoes and the button-down shirts? These are much more cumbersome to produce than the rubber clogs, because they require manual stitching, assembly, and so forth. More production complexity and manual labor equals slower production and higher costs.

Innovation using Croslite. If we were to boil down Crocs' core competency tree to a core product, it would probably be Croslite, because many (not all!) of its end products, even today, are based on this unique and proprietary material. Whereas competitors are imitating Crocs' end products of rubber clogs, they are not doing so using Croslite material. Here is an opportunity for Crocs to build on its strengths.

If we consider Crocs' core product to be the Croslite material, we see that some of the end products simply don't fit: leather and cloth shoes, cotton shirts, and indeed, CitiesByFoot.com. We can even rely on our handy Product–Market Growth Matrix (figure 8.4) to justify cutting out some of these extraneous product lines.

Market penetration. With its rubber clogs, Crocs has engaged in some co-branding with sports and entertainment companies, including NFL teams and Marvel Comics. In addition, Crocs offers different models that can span the seasons, including those with synthetic fur lining. And finally, Crocs and its retailers engage in discounting.

Market development. Crocs sells its shoes around the globe, having had more success in some markets than in others. It has also targeted its basic rubber clogs toward the medical profession (e.g., doctors, nurses) through its www.crocsrx.com site. While its market development initiatives entailed more risk than its market penetration, Crocs has been largely successful in finding new markets to sell its rubber clogs.

Product development. The Jibbitz decorative shoe attachments are geared toward kids who want to accessorize their shoes, so as a product

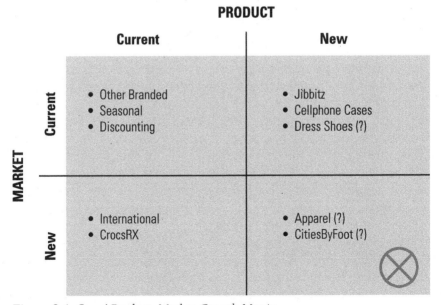

Figure 8.4. Crocs' Product–Market Growth Matrix

development initiative, this makes sense. As for Crocs' cell phone holders, though not everyone may want to accessorize their clogs, the holders are indeed made of Croslite material. But when we consider non-Croslite dress shoes, the warning bells go off. First, do customers who reach for Crocs' Croslite-based shoes want a leather shoe option from the same company? Second, where does Crocs encounter more competition, in its Croslite-based shoe business or in its leather shoe business?

Diversification. Finally, the apparel and CitiesByFoot.com expansions involve the highest risk. Without anything to differentiate its non-Croslite apparel products, Crocs faces an inordinate amount of competition from apparel marketers large and small. Similarly, its venture into the travel site business is the biggest stretch. Imagine Travelocity, a travel site, getting into the shoe business. Huh? By the way, don't bother to visit www.cities byfoot.com; Crocs quietly shut down the site.

Now that we have determined what Crocs should offer in its lineup of products, you are probably asking: What should Crocs do to continue growing? Here, we want to take cues from a successful company called W. L. Gore & Associates. You may not be familiar with the name, but you most likely know one of its products: Gore-Tex, the waterproof and breathable fabric found in rain jackets. W. L. Gore is a private corporation that specializes in the manipulation and innovation of fluoropolymers for demanding environments. Said simply, it develops and makes really cool materials that resist a lot of wear and tear. Its materials are used in planes, on oil rigs, in computers, and in medical applications—the list goes on. In fact, the company's Gore-Tex division that sells into the apparel market is just a small part of the overall business. The company's core competency tree is shown in figure 8.5.

Crocs can learn many things from W. L Gore. Just as W. L Gore isn't only a manufacturer and marketer of jackets based on its Gore-Tex material, Crocs should not see itself as only a shoe company—or a shirt company, a hat company, or a travel site company. Instead, its core competency, based on a core product, its proprietary and patented Croslite material, should involve manipulating and innovating Croslite for relevant applications. What are those relevant applications? Any activity that requires a mate-rial that is *lightweight, antimicrobial, odor-resistant,* and *nonmarking,* such as bike helmets, flatbed liners for pickup trucks, spa pillows, wheelchair pads and cushions, . . . the list goes on.

Take a look at Crocs' core competency tree (figure 8.6), not as it is today, but as it could be, based on our reconceptualized core compe-tency. Pretty neat! Unfortunately, Crocs announced on October 6, 2008, the sale to a Canadian company of all of its rights to the use of Croslite

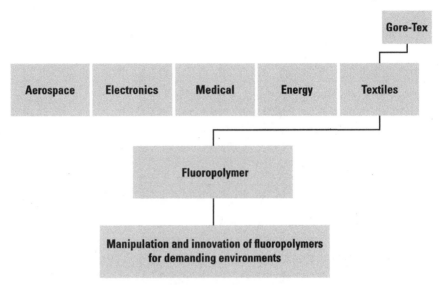

Figure 8.5. W. L. Gore's Core Competency Tree

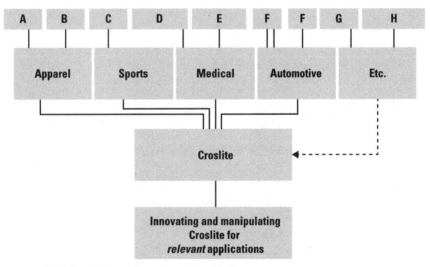

Figure 8.6. Crocs' New Core Competency Tree

material other than for shoes.[8] According to the press release, then CEO Ron Snyder viewed this transaction as a *win-win* situation because it allowed Crocs to strategically focus on its core business: Crocs branded footwear.

Win-win?

International Strategy: Stepping Out of Your Domestic Market

This workshop tackles some of the strategic considerations you need to take into account when eyeing opportunities abroad. With all the talk about the globalized marketplace, you may feel compelled to take your business international out of the gate. But wait. Before you do so, we want to provide you with some tools that can help you better evaluate opportunities. Whether you plan to source products/services or labor from a foreign country or to sell your products and services abroad, doing business internationally is an extensive, exhaustive, and often complicated process. To help you begin to make sense of how to approach the global landscape, we provide you with insights into why, when, where, and with whom you should make your strategy international. Because of all the ins and outs of doing business in a foreign country, we can only scratch the surface here. However, by the end of the workshop, you should have a firmer grasp on whether stepping out of your domestic market fits your company's overall strategy, and if so, how to begin to evaluate opportunities abroad.

The Product–Market Growth Matrix in the previous workshop mentioned, in passing, international expansion. As you drill deeper into the strategic implications of an international expansion, you will again conduct an industry analysis (using P-E-S-T-E-L, SWOT, generic strategies, Five Forces, and the value system) as well as try to understand the processes, resources, and capabilities (value chain, core competencies) that can provide a competitive advantage. That said, there is one other critical element that you need to take into consideration: country-specific benefits and drawbacks. Your international strategy will depend wholly on your understanding all three elements of your strategic inquiry: the competitive dynamics in the foreign market, the extent to which your firm-specific advantages hold up in that foreign market, and the risks and returns inherent in doing business in the specific country you target. Let's focus on how to get a handle on country-specific benefits and drawbacks.

Where should you go? That's a great question. With approximately two hundred countries around the world, you have plenty of choices for where you want to do business. How do you decide? First things first. Start by identifying optimal locations *independent* of your company's specific industry. That is, which countries are currently enjoying economic growth and prosperity? Which ones have an environment conducive to doing business internationally? North Korea? Not so much. The popular ones right now are Brazil, Russia, India, China, and South Africa (referred to as BRICS) or even Mexico, Indonesia, South Korea, and Turkey (MIST).[1] Much of their popularity comes from their status as developing countries, or economies that are shifting from an agricultural base to an industrial one. This shift toward industrialization in these countries is resulting in rising standards of living, better education for the masses, investment in infrastructure and technology, and so forth. Developed countries, in contrast, have segued from an industrial economy to a service economy. These include Japan, Germany, Canada, and the United States, among others, whose dominant industries today include software, financial services, retail, and real estate. (Agriculture makes up just 1 percent of the U.S. GDP.)[2]

The next step is to imagine the whole planet as one giant value system. Rare is the company in today's economy that hasn't felt the effects of globalization. So, just as an industry value system can help you map the various participants bringing a product or service to market, a global value system will give you a sense of which country does what. Figure 9.1 presents a simplified global value system. Commodity inputs such as coffee beans, copper, and even gold—products that are either grown or mined—make up the economies of less developed countries, whereas more developed countries focus on innovation, retailing, and services.

Recall that in Workshop 4 we laid out the value system for the PC industry. While we identified all the relevant players—from raw material providers to component suppliers to the electronic assembly firms, and beyond—we did not specify where around the globe you might find those participants. For example, the copper necessary for copper plating in a printed circuit board (PCB) may well be sourced in South America (yes, the United States still has active copper mines, but low labor costs have moved the lion's share of the production to less developed economies). Components such as power cables, which are a relatively low-tech part of the entire unit, come from India, whereas the final assembly will most probably occur in China. The channel? Walmart, Best Buy, Staples, and so

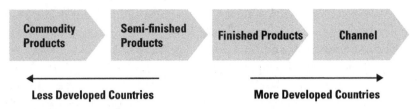

Figure 9.1. The Global Value System

forth, all of which serve the number one PC consumer market, the United States.[3] You can see how the global value system prompts you to pinpoint which country participates where in a particular industry. However, it doesn't tell you why. That is, why do certain countries produce certain products and services in the global value system? To answer this question, let's turn to Michael Porter's Diamond of National Advantage.[4]

The Diamond of National Advantage

The diamond's basic premise is that, just like companies, countries also can have core competencies. Economists traditionally assumed that a country's core competency was predicated on its factor or input conditions: the bigger the country's geographic assets, the stronger its competitive footing. Other factor conditions include population size, access to natural resources, proximity to trade routes, and so forth. However, Porter expanded this limited view to include other dynamics that help explain what makes certain countries "stick out" in the global marketplace. Take a look at the diamond in figure 9.2.

Before we put Porter's Diamond of National Advantage into action with a few examples, let's break down each of its components.

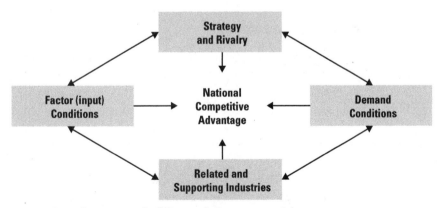

Figure 9.2. The Diamond of National Competitive Advantage

Factor conditions: As just mentioned, factor (input) conditions represent the basic factors of production, including geographic and population size, access to raw materials and skilled labor, and a country's basic infrastructure (e.g., roads, electricity, ports).

Demand conditions: Aside from the supply-side factor conditions of a particular country, it's important to understand the demand-side dynamics by exploring the nature of the home-market demand for a particular industry's product or service. That is, what are the needs and wants of a country's consumer base for a particular product or service? What does this consumer base value in those products or services? Quality? Quantity? Both? In turn, how much pressure do these consumers exert on companies to invest and innovate to satisfy those demands?

Strategy and rivalry: Once you understand the nature and extent of product or service demands of the home-market customers, you need to turn your attention to the group of companies attempting to satisfy those demands. In addition to the number of competitors vying for the customer's pocketbook, you also want to look at the overall industry structure and gain insight into how companies within that industry are created, organized, managed, and supported to satisfy consumer demands.

Related and supporting industries: You want to extend your analysis beyond just the rivals in a particular industry and explore related and supporting industries that help these rivals succeed. Supporting industries can help rivals succeed by offering more cost-effective inputs, spurring innovation, streamlining production, speeding up product launches, and so forth. Government also plays a significant role in a nation's competitiveness, because its policies can help or hinder the environment for doing business. Indeed, no one company or, by extension, one country, can reach global competitiveness without a strong network of supporting industries.

Examples of National Competitive Advantages

Let's give Porter's framework a spin to see how it handles the road. What is the biggest car company in the world?

In 2013, Japan's Toyota once again clocked in at number one, surpassing both General Motors and Volkswagen.[5] But Toyota isn't the only Japanese car manufacturer. Try to name a few more, and you'll quickly see that the list grows: Honda, Mazda, Nissan, Mitsubishi, Subaru, Isuzu, and Suzuki. Not bad for a country the size of the state of Montana!

Why is it that Japan reigns supreme in the automotive industry worldwide? Japan's endowed resources are relatively scarce. It imports most of its raw materials, such as steel and petroleum. Although as an island, the country has extensive access to ocean, the inland territory, consisting of mountains and hills, can be quite difficult to traverse. Its relatively small landmass, coupled with a population of over 120 million people (compared to 315 million inhabitants in the United States), brings its share of headaches due to space constraints.[6] Taken together, Japan's factor conditions make it difficult to understand not just its sheer number of automotive manufacturers, but also its competitive advantage in cars around the world.

Demand conditions. You can look toward the Japanese consumer to provide you with another layer of insight. Traditionally, Japanese consumers have been very discriminating when it comes to both quality and price, favoring high-end department stores over low-priced retailers for their purchases.[7] In addition, as a consumer group, they give precedence to product quality, service, display, and presentation, with cost taking a backseat. Tiny living spaces pose another problem; products have to be relatively small to fit. This extends to cars as well, given Japan's narrow roadways and postage-stamp-sized parking lots. And because of Japan's relatively high prices for gasoline, consumers demand engine technology that provides better gas mileage. We can continue to list other factors, but these give you a sense of Japan's demand conditions that provided the fertile ground for automotive manufacturers to grow.

Strategy and rivalry. We already listed the numerous carmakers in Japan. Of importance is to keep in mind that the intense rivalry (and, in many cases, collaboration) among and between these manufacturers, over the decades, has spurred continuous innovations and improvements. When considering additional growth opportunities, those carmakers rising to the top opportunistically began to eye international markets, including Honda's entry into the United States, which we discussed in Workshop 6.[8] Today, some of these brands are more prevalent in certain parts of the world, so whereas Toyota and Honda favor selling their cars in markets in advanced economies, Suzuki pursues market share in developing markets such as Southeast Asia and Africa.

Related and supporting industries. Much of Japan's culture is driven by its traditions. Given its isolationist history, especially from the early 17th century to the mid-1800s, Japan followed a model of economic self-sufficiency and interdependency. Japanese entities entering into relationships are used to taking a long-term view. This approach extends to buyers and sellers, such as Toyota's fifty-plus-year relationship with Akebono, a manufacturer of car brakes. These associations usually become formalized into interlocking shareholdings among companies, known as *keiretsu*, so that the parties are in it for the long haul, through thick and thin.[9] Because of these strong ties, one party will be induced to help the other in order for them both to succeed. Finally, Japan's government has also played a role in deciding the fate of the automotive industry, first by making car manufacturers part of the war effort and then, after the war and under American occupation, giving them the freedom and support to help rebuild the country's economy.

What we want to stress here is that *history matters* when trying to home in on a country's national competitive advantage. Think about the following countries' particular strengths on the global economic stage:

- Switzerland
- Israel
- China
- India
- United States

Switzerland. In addition to mouth-watering chocolate, Swiss-made precision watches probably came to mind. Why watches, though? Did the Swiss people wake up one day and say, "Hey, which product categories haven't yet been taken by other countries?" Not likely. The answer is one word: history. In the mid-1500s, as the Protestant Reformation swept through Europe, a Swiss pastor by the name of John Calvin took up the movement and pushed through reforms banning the wearing of jewelry, because it stood for excessive extravagance. What were you to do if you were a jeweler? Make watches, the closest product still acceptable under the new laws. The combination of consumers being allowed to wear only watches and jewelers competing for the watch market set the focus on quality and innovation for centuries.[10]

Israel. Israel has one of the highest numbers of companies listed on the Nasdaq stock exchange among non-U.S. countries.[11] Most of those companies are involved in networking and communications. Why? Because Israel relies on its networking and communications technology for its national security. Indeed, because it regularly engages in armed conflict with its neighboring countries, Israel gets to test all of its technology. Furthermore, military service is mandatory for both Israeli men and women, which makes for a highly trained workforce that understands how to translate military technology into commercially viable products.

China. Nowadays it's difficult to find consumer products that don't come with a "Made in China" label. Indeed, the saying "many hands make little work" applies. The combination of a population of over 1.3 billion, low labor wages, mass migration from the countryside to manufacturing centers such as Shenzhen and Chengdu, and a communist government that embraces industry make China a go-to destination for consumer product companies seeking cheap and fast production and assembly services. Other Asian countries such as Indonesia, Thailand, and Vietnam are also jumping on this bandwagon to take advantage of the consumerism in developed countries.[12]

India. Interested in outsourcing your back office processes, such as customer service, document management, or even software coding? If so, India remains one of the top destinations. Companies such as British Airways, American Express, and General Electric all have sourced labor-intensive yet cost-effective services from India's BPO (business process outsourcing) companies. Like China, India has a huge population (1.2 billion people), low labor wages, and a pro-business government. However, unlike China, which focuses on making and assembling hard goods (products), India's focus is on data services. Why the focus on services? History. India, as a colony of the British Empire from the mid-1800s until it achieved independence in 1947, adopted English as one of its two official languages (Hindi is the other). An educated workforce that can read, write, and speak in English can answer the phones of a call center, write software code, and even reconcile your accounting books at a fraction of the cost of U.S. labor wages.

United States. The "Great Recession" that hit the United States in late 2007 amplified the ongoing dialogue about America's global competitiveness. Questions such as "What does the United States still do best?" and "What key resources and capabilities should we nurture?" were at the heart of this debate. Michael Porter joined the debate, appearing on the November 10, 2008, cover of *BusinessWeek* with the headline, "Why America Needs an Economic Strategy." In taking a core competency view of the United States, Porter made the case that the country still offers an unparalleled environment for entrepreneurship and commercialization of innovation. In addition, it still draws much global talent to its leading educational institutions. And the government's commitment to competition and free markets, coupled with an efficient investment infrastructure that can deliver industries their capital needs, still makes for very fertile ground to grow and cultivate world-class competitors.

Just as we highlighted the importance of industry value systems in Workshop 5, it is critical for you to know the players in the global value system, those that can help you as well as those that represent a potential chokepoint to your business. If you anticipate competing on cost, you will want to source low-cost product or service inputs from countries with expertise in those particular inputs. However, if you plan to compete on uniqueness and differentiation, you will seek out partners in those countries whose national competitive advantage is based on innovation. To get a clear picture of the potential advantages and pitfalls of doing business in a particular country, you will need to start out with an in-depth P-E-S-T-E-L analysis. Although much of the information needed to fill out a country P-E-S-T-E-L is available online and through government agencies such as the U.S. Department of State and country-specific embassies and consulates, nothing beats firsthand experience and exposure in the country you are targeting. Buy that plane ticket, pack a good pair of walking shoes, and get lost among the people you want to do business with.

Foreign Market Entry Strategies

Having identified a target country, you can now transition your analysis to finding ways to strategically enter the foreign market. Figure 9.3 offers a simple yet effective framework to think through the various modes of foreign market entry. Note that the level of your company's investment, ownership, and managerial commitment increases as you move from left to right.

Exporting strategies: The least-involved approach to getting your product abroad is through exporting. Even within exporting, there are varying levels of commitment. On one end, you can hire an independent export management company (EMC) that will fill out all the necessary paperwork (licensing, customers, regulatory, tax), arrange all the transportation, help identify potential buyers, and even take possession of your goods and help market and sell them. Some of these will work on a commission basis, whereas others will be fee based. The reason that the level of ownership and investment is lower at this end of the spectrum is that you are entrusting the export merchant with your goods at the port of departure. The loss of control also increases your risk: Will the goods arrive at

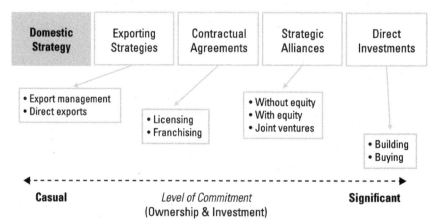

Figure 9.3. Modes of Foreign Market Entry

their destination in one piece? Will the EMC put in the effort necessary to market, distribute, and sell the goods in the foreign market? Will you actually get paid on any sales? To mitigate some of these potential concerns, you can decide to engage in direct exports yourself, although the level of involvement increases substantially.

Contractual agreements: Entering into licensing and franchising agreements with partners in a foreign market provides for much more control over how your products or services are branded, promoted, distributed, and sold. For example, Playboy Enterprises, publisher of *Playboy* magazine, has over two dozen international editions in markets such as Germany, Brazil, and the Czech Republic. To launch these editions, Playboy Enterprises enters into licensing agreements with publishers in foreign markets that dictate specific terms for publishing foreign editions, both in design and content, in an effort to preserve the iconic *Playboy* brand. This level of commitment is more involved in terms of the time, oversight, and monetary investment for the company seeking a licensing, franchising, or subcontracting relationship.

Strategic alliances: In the previous workshop on value systems, we described a strategic alliance as a relationship between two organizations involving the pooling of resources to create new products, processes, distribution channels, promotional opportunities, and so forth. When eyeing international opportunities, a company in the domestic market may want to consider entering into a partnership with a company in the foreign market. These partnerships can extend to partial equity participation in the foreign market entity. That is, the domestic company may take an ownership position in the partner company abroad. Alternatively, the two companies can enter into a joint venture to form a separate entity, with each company contributing resources (e.g., capital, employees, know-how) to this newly formed entity.

Direct investments: The most involved foreign market entry is direct investment, also known as foreign direct investment (FDI). Companies taking the FDI route can either purchase, outright, a company in another country, or they can "greenfield," from the ground up, their presence abroad. Though the resource commitment and time involvement for FDIs are extensive, so is the control of the process. One of India's largest steel companies, Tata Steel, bought Anglo-Dutch steelmaker Corus Group in 2006 in an effort to get a European footprint for steel production.[13] The acquisition cost over $12 billion; now, that's a commitment!

The foreign market entry framework brings to mind an old riddle: In a bacon-and-egg breakfast, what's the difference between the chicken and the pig? The chicken is involved; the pig is committed.

Strategy in Action: Walmart Enters India

It seems that nowadays every company wants to do business in India, whether it's sourcing the country's affordable BPO services or selling into a growing and increasingly affluent consumer market. In 2006, Walmart announced its intention to enter the Indian market and take a chunk of the $200 billion retail industry.[14] This is easier said than done. Although Walmart's opportunities in the Indian market are enormous, so are the challenges when attempting to crack this nut. We first take you through the good, the bad, and the ugly of trying to participate in India's retailing market. Once you have a grasp of the country-specific dynamics in retailing, we walk you through Walmart's particular foreign market entry strategy. As you will note, Walmart's entry mode takes into consideration many of the risks related to the Indian retailing industry.

The good: In the United States, Walmart services over 100 million customers a week, just under one-third of the U.S. population. Imagine Walmart getting 30 percent of India's 1.2 billion inhabitants as customers; that would be a whopping 400 million customers, more than the *entire* U.S. population! Over the past two decades, rapid urbanization, rising living standards, and liberalization of the Indian economy have combined to energize the country's "organized"—or modern—retail sector, which includes malls, supermarkets, hypermarkets, and specialty retailers. Global product brands such as Levi's, Benetton, Starbucks, and Nokia have firmly established their presence in India. In addition, mall store formats are becoming increasingly popular; whereas India's first mall, inaugurated in Mumbai in 1999, drew crowds not for shopping but for its air conditioning, the country today sports over three hundred malls, located mostly in urban and suburban areas.[15] The organized retailing sector is on track to grow by 40 percent year over year. It's easy to see why Walmart is licking its chops.

The bad: But hold on. Let's put this rosy outlook into perspective. For starters, take a closer look at India's population. The majority (70 percent) of its inhabitants live in the countryside, where access to drinking water, sanitation, and technology is still limited. Furthermore, literacy rates drop precipitously in rural areas, to approximately two out of every three individuals. On top of that, over a full third of the country's population is currently under fifteen years of age, which makes for *eventual* but not current shoppers. You also want to consider the country's household income statistics. More than 30 percent of India's population lives below the poverty line, making $1.25 per day (to put this in perspective, the U.S. price for a tall daily blend at Starbucks is $1.45).[16] Though the organized retail sector may be growing at 40 percent year over year, it still represents only 3 percent, or about $6.4 billion, of the overall market .[17] The other 94 percent of sales goes to *kiranas*, or mom-and-pop-style, 500-square-foot convenience stores with average overall sales of $7 *per day*.[18] In effect, these kiranas are small-scale stands that sell the day's necessities, from detergent to chewing tobacco to dry goods to bottles of Pepsi. Indeed, most Indian consumers place a heavy emphasis on consumer familiarity with local stores. That is, they like to shop with people they know, where they can get the day's gossip and, most important, bargain down the price of anything they want and need to buy. When's the last time you tried bargaining at Walmart's checkout counter?

The ugly: From the viewpoint of operating a nationwide retail chain in India, numerous additional obstacles stand in the way. Although geographically India is one country, it nevertheless comprises a vast amalgamation of languages, cultures, ethnicities, and beliefs. For example, Hindi and English are the country's official languages. However, another fourteen languages (e.g., Bengali, Tamil, Urdu, Punjabi) are spoken in various parts of the nation. Throw in local dialects, and we are looking at literally hundreds if not thousands of spoken languages.[19] Imagine the challenges in consumer communications (e.g., advertising, promotions, customer service)! This cultural fragmentation spills over into local politics as well. India's communist parties, CPI and CPIM, continue to have significant influence in certain regions, including West Bengal and Tamil Nadu. Trying to do business in these regions creates a tremendous red tape of permits, licensing, and regulations, in turn making bribery a common practice for getting business done. Another factor standing in the way of large-scale retailers is that India to this day lacks a sophisticated transportation infrastructure. Only a handful of highways exist, with the remainder being dirt roads that will leave you white-knuckled when navigating them. As an example of the logistical problem, in the United States, a trucker can haul a load one thousand miles in approximately twenty hours. The same trip in India takes five days.[20] Finally, in an effort to give its homegrown retailers a competitive advantage, the Indian government prohibits foreign retailers from making full direct investments into the country, instead forcing them into partnerships with Indian companies.

When you take all these factors into consideration, you quickly come to the conclusion that although the market potential for foreign retailers eyeing the Indian retail industry certainly exists, any player attempting to gain a toehold will face a slew of hurdles.

How Walmart Entered India

Workshop 6 identified Walmart's core competencies as its technological sophistication, which permits the company to know which products to stock when and where; its logistics infrastructure, which quickly and efficiently moves those products from vendors to shelves—and back, if they don't sell—and its sheer size, which allows the company to get price concessions from its multitude of vendors. When considering Walmart's planned entry into the Indian retailing market, it quickly becomes apparent that its core competencies are not easily or smoothly transferable. For example, Walmart's reliance on the bar code for product tracking, restocking, pricing, and so forth won't work in kiranas, because these stands don't have bar code readers. With regard to logistics infrastructure, the sheer chaos on the roads of India's cities and countryside (be prepared to swerve around stray cows!) throws a giant monkey wrench into Walmart's efficiency machine of getting products to customers where and when they want them. The only core competency left for Walmart to leverage is its size for sourcing products from vendors.

Figure 9.4 details Walmart's solution to the Indian retailing conundrum. To begin with, in 2007 Walmart entered into a joint venture with Bharti Enterprises, to circumvent the laws prohibiting direct foreign investments by retailers. As one of India's largest conglomerates, with businesses in telecommunications, insurance, real estate, food and beverage, and, yes, retailing, Bharti already had a firm grasp on how to market and sell products to the Indian consumer. The jointly formed store, called Best Price, is akin to a Costco, in that it sells bulk items in a warehouse setting, although all transactions are cash only. But here's the beauty of the relationship: rather than sell everyday goods directly to the end consumer, Best Price sells its goods to kirana stores, millions and millions of them! It's a win-win-win scenario. Walmart uses its muscle to get price concessions on detergent, chewing tobacco, dry goods, and bottles of Pepsi from its

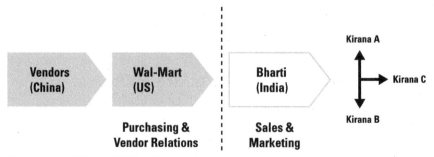

Figure 9.4. Walmart's Value System in India

vendor network; Bharti leverages its understanding of what Indian consumers want and need; and the kiranas do the day-to-day selling in their respective local neighborhoods. Whereas one kirana may achieve only $7 of sales per day, multiple transactions are generated across millions of kiranas in a 1.2 billion-consumer market. It seems Walmart has cracked the code once again.

Workshop Takeaway

The Product–Market Growth Matrix can help you evaluate when to go abroad. In this workshop, we tackled issues of where and how. Begin by visualizing the global marketplace as one giant value system: Which countries do what to bring a product or service to market? Porter's Diamond of National Advantage can help answer why certain countries focus their efforts on those products or services. Once you have a clear understanding of where you may want to source or sell your products and services, you have a spectrum of foreign market entry strategies available. Some of those strategies will require much deeper time and resource commitments than others, but their related payoffs may also be higher. As you explore your international expansion potential, keep in mind that you'll need to loop back to square one: What is the external environment of the new market? Which forces in the new market undermine your profit potential? Who is kicking and kissing whom in the new market? How can you streamline your value chain to deliver on your generic strategy of (focused) cost leadership or (focused) differentiation? And last, how well do your core competencies hold up in the new market?

Measuring Strategic Success: It Ain't a Strategy If You Can't Measure It

One of the most overlooked aspects of crafting strategy is the need to define and set objectives. In many organizations, objectives and strategy are akin to a chicken-and-egg dilemma. Which comes first? Some strategists will set objectives first, followed by strategy formulation. For example, a company may define its objective as selling an additional thousand widgets per quarter, subsequently crafting a market penetration or market development strategy to attain that particular objective. In contrast, other companies may develop a new product launch, subsequently deciding on the objectives necessary to achieve that strategy. Neither way is right. Rather, it is important to have well-defined objectives reflect the company's strategy, and vice versa. To help set your objectives, this workshop introduces you to the S.M.A.R.T. framework. As you will see, the purpose of conducting a S.M.A.R.T. analysis is to make sure your objectives align with the strategy you have crafted using the previous workshops.

Before moving on, we want to clarify the differences among goals, strategies, and objectives with a simple example. Scott's goal is to lose weight. His strategy? Begin exercising, eat more healthfully, and decrease work-related stress. His objectives? Hit the gym three times a week, switch to a Paleo diet, and leave work at the office. Although goals, strategies, and objectives are intertwined, you can see that objectives break down the strategy into workable and measurable pieces. Indeed, objectives are crucial, in that they provide benchmarks for assessing the effectiveness of a particular strategy. You'll recall from Workshop 1 that the overall effectiveness of a strategy is measured in the company's profitability. That said, objectives provide the measurable milestones that help you evaluate if you are indeed on course to reach that profitability. Furthermore, objectives ensure that everyone in your company is rowing in the same direction. Large companies with multiple divisions and management layers, as well as small start-ups in which individuals wear many hats, can often have difficulties coordinating all their employees' actions. By setting objectives, employees have an easier time taking aim and determining their own means for achieving those objectives. Apart from the concrete milestones offered by objectives, they also serve a symbolic purpose. That is, though formal in nature, they can be quite informal in how they work. For example, take chats around the water cooler. They usually intensify toward the end of a quarter or fiscal year as employees congregate to see if objectives are going to be met. Did the company achieve its sales numbers? Was the project completed on time? How many new clients came through the door? If not, who dropped the ball? Was there an external reason? Well-defined objectives help frame a crucial dialogue among employees up and down the ranks.

Now that you understand where objectives fall into the strategist's toolkit, it's important to note that there are do's and don'ts when it comes to objective setting. We begin with the don'ts, then move you to the do's with the S.M.A.R.T. framework.

Ten "Don'ts" of Objective Setting

Time and time again, we see strategists misconstruing the purpose and process of objective setting. So we compiled a top ten list to help you avoid spinning your wheels:

1. *Don't confuse goals for objectives.* We already distinguished among goals, objectives, and strategies, but we want to drive home the importance of not mixing and interchanging objectives and goals. Goals are big-picture outcomes. Objectives are the incremental means to get there. Whereas if you realize objectives, goals will take care of themselves, the opposite is never true: setting any goal will not help realize objectives. Think of goal realization as a by-product of achieving objectives: if you set the right objectives, then they will fall like dominoes, and the goal will be realized.
2. *Objective setting is not a solitary endeavor.* If you are going to set an objective for an individual or team, those people need to have some say in the objective's scope. Now, a counterargument could be made that employees will inevitably set a low bar. It's easier to underpromise and overdeliver than the other way around. That said, if people in your company are truly vested in its strategic success, they will contribute vital insights on the objectives necessary to achieve that success.
3. *Objectives are not moving targets.* One of the worst mistakes you can make as a strategist is to "move the goalposts," to borrow a phrase from American

football. An example is changing a sales quota to make it appear that the team hit the objective. The problem with such an action is that it doesn't allow for introspection. Why didn't the sales team hit the target? Is there a problem with the product? Its marketing? Did the sales team lack the proper incentive structure? Don't move the goalposts. Figure out what isn't working and why.

4. *Objectives are not private matters.* It's often the case that managers like to keep objectives close to the vest. Why? Because objectives make people accountable. But strategists often lose out on a great opportunity to get everyone on the same proverbial page. Objectives should be part of your communications strategy to key stakeholders, especially employees and investors. Strategy implementation is a tricky endeavor in its own right; foregoing the vital objective-setting dialogue with the people who can help you achieve it increases the chances of strategic failure.

5. *Objective setting is not a "let's see how we go" endeavor.* Some strategists believe in the notion of the emergent objective: roll out the strategy, see the results, then set the objectives. This is especially true with new product and new market strategies. However, the exact opposite should be your modus operandi. Start out by setting the objective, even if it means not reaching your anticipated objectives. Remember, when failing to reach an objective, smart strategists take the opportunity to ask "Why?", subsequently making the necessary strategic changes for the next performance cycle.

6. *Objectives should not benchmark solely against the past.* The laziest way to develop and set objectives is to look at last year's. The problem with such an approach is that it doesn't allow for changing business conditions. In other words, the past informs the future . . . but only up to a point. For example, take the fallout associated with the most recent recession in 2008: with consumer confidence beginning to crumble in 2007, and the effects of the economic downturn lasting well into 2010, setting objectives based on the 2007–2010 timespan would have caused any strategist to lose out on the eventual economic upswing. Our own research on managing through recessionary environments shows that many companies miss the starting gun when business recovers and subsequently are at a competitive disadvantage for years to come.[1]

7. *Objectives should not only benchmark against your company, direct competitors, or even your industry.* When setting objectives, push yourself to consider alternate company and industry viewpoints. This will keep you from setting objectives that can be myopic and in some cases even destructive to your company. Let's look at the personal computer industry again. Setting and measuring objectives in terms of PCs sold—inside the company, in relation to rivals, and in terms of the overall industry—would miss the bigger picture that the PC industry is headed for extinction. Similarly, Kodak owned the consumer photo film industry, enjoying the leading share in a market that shrank to nothing in a span of a decade.

8. *Objective setting is not solely a top-down approach.* Relying on rule by decree when setting objectives can throw strategy implementation into disarray. You

may feel inclined to blanket the company with the objective of an overall growth rate of 10 percent, with the underlying logic that for the company to grow by 10 percent, so must each revenue-generating business unit. Here's the problem: some business units will have had growth rates of 2 percent in the prior year, while others had rates in the double digits. How do you reconcile these differences with purely top-down objectives? When building and setting your objectives, rely also on a bottom-up approach that takes into account business unit variances across your company.

9. *Objectives should not work against each other.* Let's say that you have set two objectives: "In the next quarter, increase year-to-date revenues by 10 percent" and "In the next quarter, increase year-to-date profits by 15 percent." Let's also assume they are valid objectives on their own. However, when you take them together, they may be completely unrealistic. Increasing revenues may require significant investment in salespeople, advertising, and other market-ing efforts, thus putting downward pressure on your profit potential. The point is that your objectives need to be aligned and reinforce each other so that they can in fact provide you with accurate dashboard gauges to measure your strategic implementation.

10. *Objectives should not look like a grocery list.* You'll recall that when crafting strategy, as important as deciding what you are going to do is deciding what you are *not* going to do. Similarly, you should focus on just a handful of clear, concise, and strategically relevant objectives. Chasing too many objectives will distract your attention and make it difficult for employees to prioritize the ones that give you a sense of whether or not you have a working strategy.

Making S.M.A.R.T. Objectives

One of the most well-known objective-setting frameworks is S.M.A.R.T.[2] The S.M.A.R.T. framework can be used at all levels of a company, from indi-viduals to teams, from business units to the overall company. In fact, taking a S.M.A.R.T. approach throughout your company will not only help avoid ambiguity about the priority of objectives, but will also sidestep the pitfalls of managing by decree that we mentioned in our top ten list of objective-setting don'ts. Following is the breakdown of the S.M.A.R.T. acronym:

S = Specific: Objectives should be tied directly to the strategy being measured. On one level, that might be the business unit or product line or even geography involved in the strategy. On another level, the objectives can be tied to activities that are central to your strategy.

M = Measureable: How will you measure whether or not you have achieved your objective? This is what the "M" is for. "M" can also stand for metric, because objectives need to reflect a concrete measure of efforts. That means that they need to be quantifiable, or something that can be represented in numbers and will not be open for interpretation. If you think back to the distinction between goals and objectives, this type of distinction is drawn out through well-defined, quantifiable metrics. Whereas "growing the business" is a goal, "growing market share by 10 percent" starts to look like an objective because the metric can be understood by everyone in the company.

A = Assignable: For objectives to be meaningful and achievable, the people who will make them happen need to take ownership of them. Those people may be an individual, a team, a department, a business unit, or even the entire organization, but responsibility and accountability ensure that everyone's skin is in the game.

R = Realistic: One of the keys to establishing objectives is to make them accessible. Your employees will easily get discouraged if objectives seem out of reach. Start small, then go big. You may be familiar with the riddle, "How do you eat an elephant? One bite at a time." In developing realistic objectives, break them down into manageable and achievable targets. To get more clarity on those targets, you can benchmark yourself against your competitors, your industry, and the business environment as a whole.

T = Time-Bound: What is the timeline for reaching your objectives so you know if your strategy is working? The obvious time frames are quarterly, biannually, and annually. However, some organizations measure strategic effectiveness on a more current, almost real-time basis. When measuring objectives, there should be checkpoints along the way.

Setting Objectives

S.M.A.R.T. is only one aspect of creating effective objectives. Strategists also need to consider their nature. Objectives fall into three broad categories: bottom-line, industry, and organization-specific.

Bottom-line Objectives

Bottom-line objectives are those that make up the average financial statement. Regardless of the industry or organization, they are pretty standard. As shown in our definition of strategy, they are inevitably linked to profitability. However, other objectives, such as efficiency and flexibility, are also important. Now, depending on the type of business—service versus manufacturing, high tech versus low tech, early stage versus mature—some objectives may be more relevant than others. The metrics we list here are by no means comprehensive, but we like to give you a sense of how they connect to crafting strategy and setting relevant objectives.

Profitability metrics measure the value created by your company. That is, how well does the company manage the transformation of inputs into outputs that customers are willing to pay for? Remember your value chain: if you are competing on cost, then the activities will emphasize efficiencies; if you compete on differentiation, the focus is on doing something different that will get customers to pay a premium for your product or service.

- *Profit margin*: On each dollar of sales, how much do you make in earnings after *all* your costs are taken into consideration? The profit margin is calculated by dividing net income (after interest payments and taxes) by revenues (overall sales).
- *Gross margin*: The calculation for gross margin is revenues minus cost of goods sold (COGS) divided by revenues. So, what does COGS involve? These are the costs of the item you're selling. If it's a pack of gum, relevant COGS are the actual gum, the packaging, and other material costs, as well as the labor and shipping directly related to that product. That is, for each dollar you make in sales, how much of that dollar goes directly to making the product you sell? The difference between the profit margin and the gross margin is that the gross margin tells you how much you need to cover your other operating expenses, including salaries, marketing and sales, utilities, and so forth.
- *Return on assets* (ROA): How efficient are you at using your company's assets to generate earnings? To get your ROA, divide net income by total assets. The ROA is especially useful when comparing your company's performance to that of competitors in your industry.

Flexibility metrics. Organizations require strategic flexibility, which is the ability to make necessary investments to respond to external and internal changes. Companies get into trouble when their financial leverage begins to limit their strategic options. You may have a great strategy, but your obligations may keep you from implementing the strategy by placing handcuffs on your company. Smart strategists keep a tab on strategic flexibility by understanding the following metrics:

- *Working capital* represents the lifeblood of the company, in that it allows for the day-to-day transformations of inputs into outputs. In effect, working capital allows your value chain to remain viable. To calculate working capital, subtract current liabilities, or what your company owes within the next twelve months, from current assets, or those assets that can be converted into cash within the same period of time. The lower the working capital, the higher the risk that the company won't be able to pay its obligations in the near future.
- *Current ratio* takes the working capital inputs and places them into a ratio to calculate the company's slack, or its breathing room to pay short-term obligations. Divide current assets by current liabilities to get a sense of the company's overall health.
- *Debt ratio* also measures financial risk by looking at the company's overall debts and assets. The calculation is total debt divided by total assets.

Bottom-line metrics are important because they provide big-picture information about the company's strategic direction. Now we discuss industry objectives.

Industry Objectives

No two industries are alike. They differ in terms of inputs, outputs, activities, human capital, competitive drivers, and stages of evolution. Not surprisingly then, different industries have unique ways of setting objectives and measuring performance. In the printing industry, for example, companies have an objective metric called reprint rate, or the percentage of printed jobs that have to be redone due to errors. Reprints affect both the bottom line and the top line: the higher the reprint rate, the higher the cost associated with the job, thereby impacting profitability. Furthermore, as reprints go up, the more likely it is that customer satisfaction will go down, which will eventually decrease revenues. There are several manufacturing departments and functions that can contribute to a reprint rate, from client account representatives who take orders to the copy designers to the folks manning the printing presses. The reprint rate drives quality control for everyone involved and provides a tangible metric to strive toward.

Each industry comprises its own set of metrics to measure its objectives. Inventory turnover, for instance, provides a critical measure in the retailing business to indicate how quickly product is moving off the shelf. In the airline business, seat occupancy ties directly to both top- and bottom-line numbers. Of importance is to learn which are the significant ones in your particular industry, because you can then incorporate them when setting your company's objectives.

Organization-Specific Objectives

Perhaps the toughest objectives to set and measure are those that are organization-specific. Throughout this workshop, we have been stressing that objectives need to reflect the unique aspects of your strategy. By extension, this means that your company can also gain competitive advantage by having unique objectives. Indeed, not all objectives should be generic to the industry within which you operate. Objectives can and should be attached to distinctive activities within your company. Here are a few interesting company-specific objectives that we have come across:

- In 2010, Alaska Airlines introduced its twenty-minute "Baggage Service Guarantee," promising travelers that their bags will arrive at baggage claim within twenty minutes of the flight's arrival.[3] If the airline exceeds that time limit, those affected by the delay are entitled to a $20 discount on future Alaska Airlines travel or two thousand bonus miles. The particular objective of reducing the wait in baggage claim may raise the bar for the ground crew, but it extends to customer service and satisfaction, as well as the flight crew's turnaround time. Pretty S.M.A.R.T.!

- Nordstrom, the high-end retailer, relies heavily on setting customer contact objectives. To maintain high levels of customer satisfaction, the company's salespeople are tasked with sending regular quarterly notes or e-mails to their customer lists. This particular objective of receiving customer feedback is specific, measureable, assignable, realistic, and time bound; just as important, it supports the strategy of differentiating in terms of excellent customer service.
- Wendy's has some of the fastest drive-thru times in the fast-food industry.[4] To accomplish this, the company continuously refines and retunes order processing, as well as the physical kitchen layout. Talk about the devil in the details: Wendy's can shave milliseconds off a customer's wait time simply by changing the door handle on a refrigerator! A millisecond here and a millisecond there, and soon Wendy's achieves its objective of reducing wait time in the drive-thru lane.

Strategy in Action: The Imagination Factory and S.M.A.R.T.

Let's conduct a more comprehensive analysis using the S.M.A.R.T. model. We will examine a start-up toy company, The Imagination Factory, to demonstrate how to break down the company's strategy and its goals into measurable objectives. The toy company has three business lines: wooden puzzles, wooden building blocks, and active toys, also made out of wood. All products are manufactured by third parties and sold to independent retailers as well as national chains such as The Learning Company. The company's generic strategy is focused differentiation, in that it develops original, next-generation toys made predominantly out of wood. Accordingly, the price of the toys is slightly higher than that for plastic toys.

The founders have stated that their primary goal over the next twelve months is to grow the business. When pressed, they state that growing the business *rapidly* is their number one objective. Well, as we detailed previously, growing the business, even rapidly, is not an objective; it's a goal. How could you refine this goal into a well-defined objective? Running it through the S.M.A.R.T. framework helps clarify:

S = *Specific*: The objective should be tied to a specific component of the strategy, such as a business unit or product line or even development team. In the case of The Imagination Factory, the founders foresee most of the industry growth potential in active toys and accordingly want to place strategic priority on growing their active toy segment (jump ropes, swing sets, etc.). Now you've been able to refine "growing the business" into a more specific strategic focus, namely "growing the active toy business unit." Not an objective yet, but you're getting closer!

M = *Measurable*: At this stage of the company's development, revenues may be seen as more important than profit. This is an important distinction because, as we stated, sometimes objectives can fight each other! The founders further refine their measurement by focusing on "units sold" rather than revenue, because different retail channels have different price points. This further refines the objective to be, "Increase the active toy business units sold through combined offline and online channels by 15 percent."

A = *Assignable*: Given its relatively smaller size, The Imagination Factory needs to think realistically about assigning responsibility for the growth objective. The company founders recognize that both operationally and symbolically, the bulk of sales efforts has to be focused on the active toy business unit. Even though they may not have a sales team fully dedicated to the growth initiative, they can nonetheless refine the objective to "Dedicate primary sales efforts to increasing the active toy business units sold by 20 percent." The company can then also tie its marketing efforts to the objective. Although its small marketing budget prevents The Imagination Factory from promoting all three business lines equally, it can still make sure to align any marketing collateral, advertising, and tradeshow budgets toward spurring sales of the active toy unit. In that way, both marketing and sales are assigned to fulfilling the objective.

R = *Realistic*: Two specific factors may influence the founders when setting objectives. For one thing, they rely on past sales numbers to decide that a 15 percent increase in active toys over the next twelve months isn't out of the realm of possibility. However, they supplement the business units' past performance by looking outside of their company and at the industry as a whole. Indeed, trends in the toy industry are showing that kids appreciate the novelty of retro toys. More important, however, their parents are pushing for these toys in an effort to get their kids away from being glued to video games. Last, with the economy rebounding, consumers (parents) are less price sensitive than in previous years. Thus, the 20 percent increase in unit sales is deemed realistic.

T = *Time Related*: Given that toy sales are highly seasonal, the founders resolve to measure the objective accordingly. Warm-weather active toys like jump ropes will peak in the spring and early summer, cold-weather active toys will see a bump around year-end. The objective is therefore further refined to read "Dedicate primary sales efforts to increasing the active toy business units sold by 15 percent through the full calendar year."

By bringing the original goal through the S.M.A.R.T. framework, we can break down the strategy and goals of The Imagination Factory into a much more concrete and actionable set of objectives. Compare the two objectives:

"Grow the business rapidly."

versus

"Dedicate primary sales efforts to increasing the active toy business units sold by 15 percent through the full calendar year."

Workshop Takeaway

As with strategy, setting objectives is a unique endeavor that should reflect your company, its position among competitors, as well as its larger goals. As we detailed, people tend to minimize objective setting in their strategic planning. More often than not, they are guilty of one of the ten "don'ts" of objective setting. Writing and setting well-defined objectives isn't easy. Not only is it time intensive, but employees often resist the process for the very simple reason that well-written objectives make them accountable. However, the S.M.A.R.T. framework, by opening up the lines of communication among the various business units, can greatly facilitate the activity of setting objectives. With your strategic ducks all in a row, you are finally ready to set off on your journey. Follow us into the next workshop, on strategic implementation.

Strategy Implementation: Getting Your Strategic Ducks in a Row

Let's reflect on all the frameworks available throughout these workshops for crafting your strategy: P-E-S-T-E-L, SWOT, generic strategies, Five Forces, value chain, value system, core competency, Product–Market Growth Matrix, Diamond of National Competitive Advantage, and S.M.A.R.T. Your toolbox is jam-packed! Up until now you have relied on these tools to sketch your strategy on a whiteboard, in a PowerPoint file, in a binder, or in a Word document. However, it has yet to see the light of day. It's time to get your hands dirty with strategic implementation! Let's draw an analogy between implementing a strategy and doing a home project.

You buy an old fixer-upper house as an investment. Looking at the neighborhood, you have a design in mind that will make the house "stick out" from other houses on the market. Indeed, you see it, not for what it is, but rather for what it can be: not only will this house be an architectural marvel, but it will also be the first one in the neighborhood that is fully LEED certified (i.e., environmentally friendly in terms of energy efficiency, materials used, etc.). You draw up specific blueprints, set a reasonable budget, hire a responsible and honest contractor, locate a source for most of your "green" inputs, and give yourself seven months to finish the job, setting milestones along the way. Time to break ground.

One of the first things you tackle is the old, outdated, and crumbling interior. However, as you begin the teardown—the process of ripping out the old walls and fixtures—the contractor finds that you have serious water damage from a leaky roof. As a result, the floor and ceiling joists will have to be replaced, which will bump up your costs. The contractor, though reputable, is going through some personal issues, which is slowing down construction. One of the few local green materials suppliers just went out of business, forcing you to find an alternate provider in another state. Your milestones are quickly running away from you. You may have had the best-laid plans, but once you began the actual execution, those plans went awry.

Our point is that crafting strategy is not unlike a home improvement project, in that once you hit the "go" button, anything can happen. Strategic plans are clean, easy, and often beautiful. Strategic implementation, on the other hand, can leave you sweaty, messy, and disheartened. To smooth the implementation of your strategy, this workshop introduces you to Michael Porter's activity maps.[1] These simple charts are meant to keep your attention on the activities that need to be accomplished on a day-to-day basis, in an effort to maintain your company's competitive advantage. You may recall from Workshop 1 the notion of fit and the need for all of the company's resources, capabilities, and activities to work together, in unison, to reinforce each other. The synergistic effect of these inner workings fitting together and running smoothly is to "lock out" competitors. With an activity map, we focus exclusively on those activities. And by getting a clear visual representation of how they link to one another, you can avoid missing critical steps of your strategic implementation.

Aligning All the Moving Parts

Strategic implementation involves a lot of moving parts. In any company of any size, whether in the aerospace, food, or pharmaceutical industries, strategic implementation is a daily endeavor of executing the various activities that make up your overall strategy. In addition to visually representing those activities, the activity map will also reflect—either implicitly or explicitly—your company's positioning, critical trade-offs you need to keep in mind, your company's unique activities, and by extension, its secret sauce and fit. To be more specific, the activity map's resulting one-page visual representation will guide you as follows:

- To what extent you employ variety-, needs-, or access-based positioning will be highlighted by the type of activities on your map and how they link to each other. For example, *where* your product is marketed and delivered may reveal an access-based positioning, whereas *whom* you market and deliver to will give you an indication of your needs-based positioning.
- Which activities are truly unique will be spelled out in black and white on the map. If you find them not to be unique, remember that you can have *similar* activities performed *differently* to lock out competitors. What this implies is that the activities may need to connect to each other in some distinctive way.

- Trade-offs become both explicit and implicit. What you *have to do* in terms of day-to-day activities is explicit, leaving those things that you are *not* going to do off the page.
- Fit is shown by linking the various activities together to demonstrate consistency and reinforcement where it exists. If, in the process, you find an activity without a link to another one, you should revisit the stray activity. It may be brought into the fold to strengthen your competitive engine. On the other hand, if it is redundant or superfluous, you can consider doing away with it.

Building Your Activity Map

Creating activity maps is a visual endeavor. We realize most of you are too busy running your business to sit down and draw, but we believe you should give it a try. Even if you produce a rudimentary activity map on a bar napkin, we think the exercise is incredibly valuable. No one's looking for a work of art. Rather, the strategic frameworks are valuable because they help refine your thinking. As an added benefit, if you produce an activity map that you can share with the troops, you'll really have something of value. As you contemplate your company's activity map, keep these factors in mind:

1. What are the strategic imperatives that make you "stick out" in the competitive market place? Hint: What's your core competency, or what do you want it to be? Draw a few big circles in the middle of the page and label them with those strategic imperatives.
2. Now start to brainstorm on a separate sheet of paper by listing the activities that support the strategic imperatives.
3. Next, overlay all these activities as they relate to your company's strategic imperatives.
4. Finally, start to detail the linkages between activities. Do you see consistency and reinforcement?

Let's build an activity map for Joe's Java Room. Joe is a local coffee entrepreneur who wants to open a coffee shop in downtown Mill City, Maine. To a large degree, his motivation to start a coffee shop is his belief that he can fill an unmet need within the community. That is, he can come in and occupy a focused yet differentiated position among Starbucks, Dunkin' Donuts, and gas stations offering on-the-go coffee. In thinking about his particular strategy, Joe builds it around four imperatives:

- World-class coffee: Java Room will offer unique flavor profiles, sourced from different parts of the world and blended just for him. Not your average cup of joe. Pun intended!

- Welcoming experience: Rather than have people run in and out or speed through drive-thrus, Joe is looking to create a community where folks can come, stay, socialize, and enjoy their time.
- Engaged employees: Joe wants his employees to feel a part of the business and to be invested in its success. Happy employees will make for happy—and returning—customers.
- Social responsibility: Joe believes increasingly that businesses should be tied to their local community, as well as the world at large. Part of his plan is to give back to the community through selective cause-related marketing. In addition, he will source coffee beans that are fair trade certified.

These strategic imperatives serve as the basis for Joe's activity map (figure 11.1).

Have we mentioned that the devil is in the details when it comes to strategic implementation? How does Joe bring his strategy to life? That is, what are the activities that will help him realize his strategy? Let's begin with employee engagement. They can't simply be hourly employees who turn over every three months. Joe needs folks who are committed to the business. In fact, he believes engaged employees are central to his focused differentiator position, because they will connect with the community and keep customers coming back. However, accomplishing this is not as simple as giving a daily "rah-rah" speech to the employees. To achieve employee engagement, Joe will have to implement some concrete, tangible practices:

- Employee health care: Aside from the social responsibility Joe feels about offering health care, he knows it's good business. If he can keep the employees on the job, then he will decrease headaches and customer dissatisfaction.
- Employee profit sharing: Joe knows that giving the employees skin in the game will motivate them to be more customer service oriented.

Figure 11.1. Joe's Java Room: Activity Map, Step 1

- Paying a living wage: Joe also knows that in retail, employee turnover— the rate of workers leaving the business—exceeds 50 percent. That is, year to year, almost half of employees leave. This makes it tough to maintain a strong customer-driven culture. Paying a living wage will be one piece of his solution.
- Empowered employees: Joe will be hands-on, but there will be times when employees have to make decisions. Joe hopes that he can build this type of empowered culture.
- Continuous training: Joe intends to bring in a services business consultant on a quarterly basis to get his employees up to speed on the latest thinking in ser-. vices innovation and customer satisfaction.

Figure 11.2 overlays these categories on the bigger activity map. Note how the map shows the relationships and reinforcements among the activities while simultaneously maintaining the larger strategy. For example, you'll see that providing your employees with continuous training, offering them a proper living wage, and allowing them to participate in profit sharing all contribute to employee empowerment, resulting in the necessary employee engagement to enhance the customer's experience. In effect, the strategic implementation around employee engagement is realized by explicitly detailing the activities and these relationships.

Figure 11.2. Joe's Java Room: Activity Map, Step 2

These are not pie-in-the-sky pursuits, but rather concrete activities that can be tied to company-specific objectives. For instance, the living wage can be set to a certain dollar amount. Similarly, profit sharing can be linked to tenure, and healthcare premiums can be identified and quantified. To reiterate, you want to make certain that these activities can be tied to S.M.A.R.T. objectives. And though you don't want have a grocery list of objectives, it is important to be able to measure strategic activities that help you compete and create value in the marketplace.

Let's tackle the Java Room's welcoming experience next. Joe believes that folks need to think of the Java Room like a library: no need to rush; stay as long as you like. As with employee engagement, the welcoming experience imperative will be realized by the implementation of some key activities:

- Free Wi-Fi: The Java Room will offer access to the Internet at no charge.
- Book clubs: Activities will be central to building community; the Java Room will hold weekly book clubs.
- Community activism: Joe will actively promote the Java Room as a meeting venue for community groups, such as school committees, art organizations, and other local nonprofits.
- Spatial feng shui: To take his customers' comfort and relaxation to a whole new level, Joe will hire a feng shui consultant to create a harmonious environment.
- Live music: Joe doesn't want the Java Room to be busy only from 6:00 a.m. to 2:00 p.m. He will try to get full utility out of his space by offering music acts and other activities to draw people in outside of traditional coffee shop hours.
- Quality furniture: The Java Room will be filled with high-quality, comfortable, durable furniture.

Figure 11.3 presents Joe's activity map, reflecting activities related to the welcoming experience. As in the previous step, the listed activities link not only directly to the welcoming experience, but also to one another. For example, the quality furniture activity supports clientele coming to congregate, relax, listen to music, or surf the Web.

We have not included detailed descriptions of the last two strategic imperatives, social responsibility and world-class coffee, but figure 11.4 shows the Java Room's complete map of the activities linking to all four strategic imperatives.

The more time you take to refine your activity map, the tighter the strategic links will become. You may also find that certain activities attach across the activity map to other strategic imperatives; consider the no-Styrofoam item and its connection to world-class coffee. To reinforce the notion that the Java Room offers world-class coffee, Joe will probably use

Figure 11.3. Joe's Java Room: Activity Map, Step 3

mugs instead of plastic cups. Similarly, though paying a living wage is central to employee engagement, it also spans the activity map to support social responsibility. These types of reinforcements are often found throughout the activity map, especially if done well.

The Human Element of Strategy Implementation

Having crafted your top-down strategy, established your S.M.A.R.T. objectives, and mapped out your day-to-day activities, you are ready to implement your strategy. But before you do, ask yourself one last but essential question: Do I have the right human capital to help implement the strategy? At the end of the day, strategy, from beginning to end, represents human endeavor. To help you determine if you have the right human organization to get you to your strategic destination, we want to address issues relating to people, culture, leadership, and incentives. All of these have their own dedicated fields of researchers and practitioners who can offer valuable and insightful frameworks and prescriptions, so our suggestions barely scratch the surface. However, our intention is to make you aware of these essential factors that can help or hinder your strategy implementation.

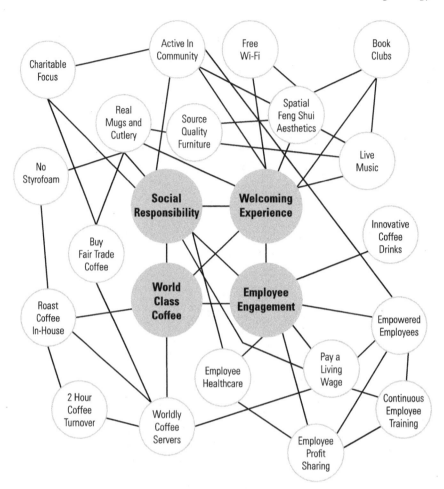

Figure 11.4. Joe's Java Room: Activity Map, Step 4

People: Making Sure Your Company Has the Right Talent

All the strategic successes or failures covered in this book are attributable to the people who made them happen, for better or worse. When you boil it down, the talent you employ embodies the competencies you need to create value for your customers. Jim Collins, management guru and author of the best seller *Good to Great*, uses a simple yet effective analogy: get the wrong people off the bus and the right ones on if you want your organization to thrive.[2] What constitutes the *right* people is not always clear; you may have employees with the right skill set, but they may not have the right attitude or core beliefs to make the strategy happen. This is often the case in companies looking to strategically redirect after having been on the same path for a long time. Some employees will resist the change, simply because they are accustomed to doing business a certain way. Of course, getting the wrong people off the bus and the right ones on can be a highly unpleasant process. But the key is to get the fitting talent in place before executing your strategy, because if the implementation fails, everyone's position in the company is in jeopardy.

Culture: "That's Not How We Do Things Around Here!"

Building on our previous point, no matter how well thought-out your strategy, if the culture within the organization doesn't support it, you have big problems. Broadly speaking, culture concerns the core values and beliefs in a company that define how business is conducted. It can be tough to pinpoint, and it varies across organizations. In thinking about the Java Room, Joe needs to cultivate a culture of passion for world-class coffee, concern for global and local social issues, entrepreneurial behavior, and dedication to the customer experience. These values, in turn, drive how Java Room employees fulfill the activities on the strategy map. They also dictate Joe's hiring, training, and even firing decisions.

Southwest Airlines offers another great example of the profound role of culture in strategy. Once Southwest established itself in the airline industry, Herb Kelleher, its founder and then CEO, worried whether the company's rapid growth would strangle the entrepreneurial and unorthodox culture that drove the airline's success to begin with. In an effort to avoid this, Kelleher formed a culture committee, enlisting employees from across the airline for two-year commitments. Kelleher called the members of this committee his "fire watchers," a term he borrowed from prehistoric times, when one lucky member of the tribe was designated to watch the fire and make sure it wouldn't go out.[3] At Southwest, these fire watchers were tasked with ensuring the "fire"—Southwest's unique culture—did not get extinguished as the company grew.

For strategy implementation to succeed, your company's culture has to be in alignment. Part of your culture can be as simple as a dress code that puts employees in the right mind-set. In the case of Zappos, the online shoe retailer, it can include the company's self-proclaimed promise of "a little weirdness" in the workplace. Take time before implementing your strategy to ask, "What is our culture?" and "Does it support what we are trying to accomplish here?"

Incentives: You Get What You Pay For

We cannot overstress the importance of relying on employee incentives when striving for successful strategic implementation. We don't mean just any kind of incentives, but rather those that best align with your overall strategy. If you think back to the Joe's Java Room example, Joe offered a living wage, profit sharing, health benefits, and continuous training to drive employee empowerment. Empowered employees, in turn, support the other strategic imperatives, such as creating new flavor blends (world-class coffee), getting involved in local community events (social responsibility) and, of course, serving a cup of coffee with a smile (welcoming experience).

Similarly, if you are planning a new product launch (product development), you need to consider the most effective compensation structure that will result in a win-win for both your sales team and your company as a whole. A sales force solely working off commission can quickly get burned out and disheartened if customers resist purchasing the new product. Alternatively, just paying base salaries offers little incentive for the sales staff to go out there and peddle the new wares.

Here is a real-world example to illustrate the potential misalignment between incentive and implementation. Sheila worked in the presales department for a major lawn service company. The department's function was to generate leads for the sales team. In line with this, Sheila's job was to cold-call homeowners to gauge their interest in the company's lawn care services. The company offered Sheila the following incentive: she would be eligible for a commission simply for getting homeowners to agree to a free lawn care estimate. For the company to confirm whether the homeowners were indeed willing to receive this free lawn care estimate, Sheila had to get them to provide the color of their house. Subsequently, if the company's sales person followed up on the presales call and found the color of the homeowner's house matched Sheila's presales report, *cha-ching*, Sheila got a commission, whether or not the sales person made an actual sale. Seems simple enough.

Well, Sheila quickly found that getting homeowners to stay on the line was not the easiest job. In fact, most people promptly hung up before she could even start on her pitch. But it didn't take Sheila long to realize that all she needed to get paid was the color of the house. So she tailored her strategic activities accordingly by calling homeowners and pretending to work for a large paint company interested in surveying the most popular exterior house colors in that particular neighborhood. It was a quick call that usually resulted in Sheila getting the information she needed; most people felt unthreatened because they weren't sold anything. You can imagine why, at the end of the summer, Sheila was the top presales person in office.

Now, this example certainly borders on the ridiculous, possibly even illegal. Nevertheless, it serves to illustrate that how you structure your incentives to achieve your strategic goals can be a double-edged sword. Remember, you get what you pay for!

Ready, Fire, Aim

What if the strategic implementation isn't working? Well, guess what? Many great strategies did not succeed at first. They often required a second and even a third iteration. Take Apple, which found itself on the verge of bankruptcy in 1997, but pivoted from being a hardware and software provider to a digital lifestyle solutions company. Strategic implementation requires flexibility, with minor tweaks, and at times, even drastic adjustments along the way.

If you're not making any headway, your first instinct may be to blame the strategy, thinking that if it's not implementable, then it's not a good strategy. That may be the case, but before pushing the reset button, take the time to review your strategy from the bottom up. Start with your strategic imperatives, activities, and related S.M.A.R.T. objectives. Are they aligned with your growth initiatives? Do they reflect your core competency? You can then continue your inquiry by revisiting your value chain to see if it's aligned with your core competencies, as well as the strategic imperatives and objectives. Keep going up the levels of your strategic analysis, and you may find that you have possible misalignments that require your attention.

Strategy in Action: Dunkin' Donuts

We have emphasized the value in building your company's activity map. However, you may also want to sketch out your direct competitors' activity maps, for several reasons. First, a comparison of activity maps will help underscore those activities that you do better, differently, or both. Moreover, you may identify some of your competitors' activities that you want to emulate and subsequently tailor to your company. After all, imitation is the sincerest form of flattery! Last, laying out your competitors' strategic imperatives and the activities that help realize those imperatives will provide you with a crystal-clear picture of their positions in the market. That is, you'll know what it means to compete as a (focused) cost leader or differentiator in your particular industry and can position your company relative to your competitors accordingly.

As an example, we build on the activity map created for Joe's Java Room, a focused differentiator, by exploring the strategic imperatives and activities of Dunkin' Donuts, a cost leader. If, at its core, strategy is about being different, then Dunkin's map of activities should look quite distinctive from that of the Java Room. Before we get to the activity map, though, let's provide a little background on Dunkin'.

Dunkin' was founded in 1950 by Bill Rosenberg as a one-location donut joint in Quincy, Massachusetts. Quickly recognizing the donut shop's potential, Rosenberg launched a franchising program in 1955 that would grow the company exponentially. Today, Dunkin' serves five million customers a day, in more than ten thousand stores worldwide, offering seventy varieties of donuts, over a dozen coffee beverages, as well as other fare. Indeed, Starbucks has a worthy competitor in Dunkin' Donuts.[4]

What accounts for this company's continued success in the crowded coffee shop and fast-food business? Dunkin' Donuts occupies a niche in the food service world, in that it owns the donut category. That said, however, the company strives to remain relevant in a changing macro-environment. Unlike its competitor, Krispy Kreme, which only sticks to donuts, Dunkin' Donuts has expanded its product offerings (product development), including iced drinks, sandwiches, wraps, and bagels, and cultivated other channels and markets, such as grocery stores and its international markets (market development). Furthermore, Dunkin' was one of the first quick-service restaurants to "break out" of its hourly confines. Given its core product offering, Dunkin' was traditionally confined to selling donuts and coffee during the early morning rush. What do you do when consumers' cravings for donuts are satisfied by 10 a.m.? Close shop? That's a lot of wasted time, resources, and store space! But keeping the doors open and counters staffed costs even more money, especially if no one's buying donuts! With management resolving to offer all-day service, Dunkin' began experimenting with additional menu offerings that could satisfy customers' lunch, snack, and dinner needs.

In addition to the strategic imperative of transforming itself into an all-day eating destination, Dunkin's three other imperatives include speed of service, location flexibility, and brand evolution. Speed of service leverages Dunkin's long-standing experience dealing with the morning rush crowd to continue its focus on quick food and beverage service. In addition to its stand-alone stores, customers can frequent Dunkin' inside Walmart outlets, on college campuses, at airports, and even in gas stations. Given the size differences in Dunkin's store formats, the company places an emphasis on location flexibility. Finally, brand evolution is a strategic priority, because Dunkin' has to reflect ever-changing consumer behaviors.

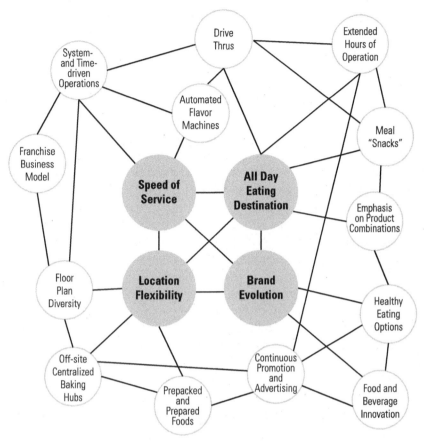

Figure 11.5. Dunkin' Donuts' Activity Map

Figure 11.5 presents Dunkin's activity map, complete with these four strategic imperatives as well as related activities.

In looking more closely at the activities, we see that they align with Dunkin's distinctive strategic imperatives. For example, by offering healthy eating options such as wraps, Dunkin' plugs into the trend of healthier eating habits. Similarly, its off-site centralized baking hubs allow the company to quickly and effectively deliver products to all of its locations, large or small. As in the Java Room example, these activities should be reinforcing. Take Dunkin's extended hours of operation and continuous promotion and advertising: one feeds the other, thereby unifying the strategic imperatives and locking out competitors.

Would the activity maps of Dunkin's primary competitors, Krispy Kreme and Starbucks, look the same? Not at all. Krispy Kreme, for example, focuses only on the product category of donuts. Consequently, both its strategic imperative and related activities look quite different. Starbucks, on the other hand, gives precedence to coffee-based beverage innovation; hence the company's claim that it offers over fifty thousand different drink combinations. Think about the activities to support that claim! Grande, nonfat, no water, Tazo chai tea latte, anyone?

Workshop Takeaway

After you put down this book, implementation will be entirely up to you! Just as strategy formulation is a unique endeavor for each company, so is strategic implementation. To help with the implementation of your strategy, draft an activity map representing your company's strategic imperatives as well as the activities that support those imperatives. As we mentioned, no matter how rudimentary, a sketched-out activity map will help pave the way to successful implementation of your strategy.

Keep in mind the importance of the human element, the folks who are going to execute your strategy. Do you have the right people in place? Is the culture conducive to the strategy you want to achieve? In terms of leadership, is it in place in both the top and middle ranks of the organization? In terms of incentives, is everyone involved in the execution properly motivated by what you're trying to achieve?

Finally, no strategy will roll out the way it was initially formulated. Instead, you will have to adapt, adjust, and improvise along the way to realize your strategy. Knowing that is half the battle.

Wrap-up: Mastering Strategy . . . and Beyond!

A well-known strategist once said: "All men can see individual tactics necessary to conquer, but almost no one can see the strategy out of which total victory is evolved."[1] These words were put to paper by Sun Tzu, a Chinese military general, in *The Art of War* more than 2,500 years ago. They show that strategy has been part of humankind's thinking and vocabulary for a long time. In fact, we suspect that strategy goes back even further, to when our ancestors Grunt and Clonk, facing down a saber-toothed cat, quickly thought through their respective options: outrun one another (efficiency) or make like a tree (innovation).

Fast-forward to the 1950s, when companies began adopting some of the strategic thinking traditionally reserved for military applications; the field of business strategy was born. Since then, researchers, academics, and practitioners have contributed extensively to the discipline, in the process giving professionals the type of tools necessary to make informed decisions about the direction of their businesses.

With *Mastering Strategy: Workshops for Business Success*, our goal has been to take the most popular and effective tools and make them accessible to you. The order of the workshops took a top-down approach: from an evaluation of the external environment to an understanding of industry-specific competitive dynamics to an assessment of core competencies and capabilities and the implementation necessary to make your company "stick out" from its competitors. We want to reiterate a few key points made throughout the book:

1. Use the frameworks in unison; together, they provide you with a comprehensive picture of your strategic challenges and opportunities. The more integrative

your strategic formulation, the lower the chances are that you will overlook some important issue that will thwart your strategic implementation.

2. Remember, as long as there are competitive dynamics at play, these tools, if applied properly, give a clear understanding of the competitive dynamics and, more important, the strategic choices available to you to navigate those dynamics.

3. As you set off to strategize for your business, don't go searching for a right strategy. Rather, keep in mind that each strategy carries with it certain risks and related returns. It all depends on what you intend to accomplish.

4. Strategy is both a science and an art. As science, the frameworks will help you immensely, but only up to a point! Like a sculptor envisioning a three-dimensional statue in a formless piece of marble, a truly great strategic thinker reaches beyond the world as it is and begins to see it as it could be.

5. The strategist is you! Whether an entrepreneur, a third-generation family business owner, a middle manager, or a seasoned executive, the need to think and act strategically falls squarely on your shoulders. Too often we hear refrains of "I'm too busy with day-to-day operations to think about strategy" or "I leave strategy to someone else, higher up."

6. Sir Winston Churchill once said: "However beautiful the strategy, you should occasionally look at the results." Indeed, strategic implementation is where the rubber meets the road, requiring a proactive, disciplined, yet nimble approach. Rather than being set in stone, strategies should have a general direction but remain organic enough to enable adjustments along the way.

Taking our last point, we suggest that strategy is 5 percent inspiration and 85 percent perspiration. We assign the remaining 10 percent to plain old-fashioned luck. It helps when the market bends to your favor, as was the good-luck case with the 1973 oil crisis and Japanese car manufacturers. And sometimes the market will move against you: think digital music and record stores.

Additional Resources

With some of strategy left to luck, outside of your control, we invoke the words of French chemist and microbiologist Louis Pasteur: "Chance favors the prepared mind." We couldn't agree more. Here are a few additional resources we believe will continue to prepare you as you set forth.

Popular Business Press

As strategic management academics, we keep our minds sharpened by reading a variety of business publications, both online and offline. Certainly there is an abundance of daily sources to choose from, including the *Wall Street Journal*, the *New York Times*, the *Financial Times*, and *Investor's*

Business Daily, among others. All of these publications provide in-depth coverage of the strategic challenges and opportunities of businesses across industries. For those of us who are time-constrained, weekly and biweekly business magazines such as *Bloomberg Businessweek, Forbes, Fortune,* and *Fast Company* provide a quick-read alternative. *Entrepreneur* magazine and *Inc.* magazine, both geared toward start-ups/small businesses, also offer extensive how-to advice and tools.

We suggest you pick one magazine that speaks to you, stylistically and in terms of content, and read it on a regular basis. As you read through articles profiling a business or an industry, try to keep in mind the strategic frameworks covered in the workshops. You will begin to see the frameworks "popping" as you bring your critical eye to the articles. The more you can exercise your strategic muscle, the better will be your ability to recognize patterns in your own company and industry.

Trade Business Press

Many of the frameworks in our workshops appeared in *Harvard Business Review*, Harvard University's magazine offering original research from some of the world's most prominent management thinkers. *MIT Sloan Management Review* is the Massachusetts Institute of Technology's business journal of a similar ilk. Both publications deliver information on the latest and greatest strategy tools in an accessible and easy-to-read manner.

Leading strategic management consulting firms such as McKinsey & Company, Boston Consulting Group, and Bain & Company also offer strategy articles, research papers, webinars, and other materials of interest, free of charge.

Finally, each industry usually has dedicated trade publications and Web sites that offer industry-specific coverage, white papers, blogs, and webcasts. Typing "trade publications by industry" into a search engine will point you in the right direction.

Business Books

Books about business come in many forms, including first-person accounts, cartoon books (think *Dilbert*), and how-to guides, like this one. We want to share a few books that have served as our go-to resources on a variety of strategy issues. With *Mastering Strategy: Workshops for Business Success* under your belt, we would like to point you toward these next three titles. Consider these "advanced strategy" readings. We explain how they build on our book.

Blue Ocean Strategy, by Renee Mauborgne and W. Chan Kim.[2] Whereas the frameworks contained in *Mastering Strategy: Workshops for Business Success* are suitable for all types of competitive situations, the authors of *Blue Ocean Strategy* place emphasis on market environments ruled by extreme rivalry. With ferocious competitors engaged in a feeding frenzy for growth and profits (hence the red ocean imagery in the book), smart companies seeking to survive and flourish need to create new demand in previously uncontested market spaces. One of the key precepts in *Blue Ocean Strategy* is that, unlike in conventional strategy, companies can and should occupy both low-cost and differentiation positions. Rather than getting stuck in the middle, these companies use value innovation to effectively uncover a side door out of the hypercompetitive space they currently face, in the process creating new, untapped markets. *Blue Ocean Strategy* offers a variety of useful tools for both start-up entrepreneurs and seasoned professionals to rethink their businesses' value propositions and reimagine the customers they serve.

Business Plan Generation: A Handbook for Visionaries, Game Changers, and Challengers, by Alexander Osterwalder and Yves Pigneur.[3] *Business Plan Generation*'s main tool, the business model canvas, is an incredibly useful framework to help you understand the engine that drives strategy: the business model. "Being different" is at the heart of strategy; that is, you want your company to stick out from the competition. How you generate revenues and, in turn, profitability, is the purview of the business model. What links the two concepts is simple. If the business model doesn't generate ample profits, the company will run out of gas, and the strategy will have been for naught. An example to drive home the connection: Facebook has a strategy: it's certainly different and unique in terms of its competitive position in the social media and networking market. However, its business model—how it will actually make money off its millions and millions of users—is still open to question. *Blue Ocean Strategy* and *Business Plan Generation* go hand in hand. Whereas *Blue Ocean Strategy* provides the tools to create a new customer value proposition, *Business Plan Generation* helps you think through different ways to make money off that proposition.

The Balanced Scorecard, by Robert Kaplan and David Norton.[4] This book provides an excellent tool for strategy implementation in the form of the balanced scorecard. We noted in an earlier workshop that if you can't measure it, you probably don't have a strategy. In addition to the tools we have provided, *The Balanced Scorecard* offers a step-by-step approach to evaluating the four most important metrics in your business: financial performance, customer value, internal business processes and productivity, and employee performance. The tool is especially useful to get everyone in a company on the same proverbial page (the balanced scorecard framework is, in fact, a one-pager). The process of prioritizing strategic goals and metrics to measure strategic implementation is as crucial as the resulting document. *The Balanced Scorecard* is widely used for strategy planning sessions in companies both large and small.

www.Mastering-Strategy.com (Our Own Resource!)

You have hung in there with us this far, but that doesn't mean we have reached the end. In fact, let us be part of your ongoing journey! Our Web site, www.mastering-strategy.com, is chock-full of strategic goodies that can help guide you down your path. Here are just a few features that we offer:

- *Strategic tools*: You can download PDFs and Word files of worksheets to use in your strategic formulation and implementation.
- *Real-time case studies*: We take business situations currently unfolding in the real world and provide our own strategic takes and insights.
- *Real-time Twitter feeds*: Follow us on Twitter as we weigh in on business situations.
- *Webinars*: Join us on topical webinars ranging from strategies for navigating economic recessions to corporate turnaround to strategic corporate governance.
- *Q&A sessions*: Interact with us and let us answer your questions concerning strategy.
- *Blogs*: Read our topic-specific blogs and find additional resources.
- *Original research*: Read our homegrown research offering prescriptive advice on your business.
- *Book reviews*: We provide in-depth reviews of business books hitting shelves and e-readers near you.
- *Teaching strategies*: For those of you who teach strategy or want to host your own seminars, we offer award-winning tips and guidance on what to teach and how to teach it.

Thank you for picking up a copy of *Mastering Strategy: Workshops for Business Success*. Don't be shy; let us hear from you!

Mike (mike@mastering-strategy.com) and Scott (scott@mastering-strategy.com)

Notes

Introduction

1. "How the AOL-Time Warner Deal Went Wrong." *Dealbook*, January 11, 2010.

Workshop 1

1. *Webster's New American Dictionary.* New York: Smithmark Publishers, 1995, s.v. "strategy."
2. *Webster's New American Dictionary*, s.v. "strategy."
3. Elliott Weiss and Anwar Harahsheh. *Southwest Airlines: Keeping That Lovin' Feeling after Herb Kelleher.* Charlottesville, VA: Darden Business Publishing, 2002.
4. Vivienne Walt. "Norway to Wal-Mart: We Don't Want Your Shares," *Fortune*, July 24, 2006.
5. Michael Porter. "What Is Strategy?" *Harvard Business Review* 74 (1996): 61–78.
6. Walter Isaacson. "The Real Leadership Lessons of Steve Jobs," *Harvard Business Review* (April 2012): 94.
7. Tom Van Riper. "Walmart Goes Upscale," *Forbes*, August 30, 2006.
8. "Why Neutrogena?" http://www.neutrogena.com/category/why+neutrogena .do.
9. Jad Mouawad. "Southwest, Determined to Expand, Buys AirTran," *New York Times*, September 27, 2010.

Workshop 2

1. Anita McGahan. "How Industries Change," *Harvard Business Review* 82 (2004): 94–104.
2. Sudeep Reddy. "Latinos Fuel Growth in Decade," *Wall Street Journal*, March 25, 2011.

3. Susan Berfield. "Why the McWrap Is So Important to McDonald's," *Bloomberg Businessweek*, July 3, 2013.
4. "Our Rich History." http://corporate.westernunion.com/History.html.
5. Willy Shih, Stephen Kaufman, and David Spinola. *Netflix,* Boston: HBS Premier Case Collection, 2007.
6. Lauren Effron. "Netflix CEO Reed Hastings Says Company Has 'Sincere Regret' Over Handling of Service Changes," *ABC News*, September 26, 2011.

Workshop 3

1. Michael Porter. *Competitive Advantage,* New York: The Free Press, 1985, 12.
2. "Our Story." http://corporate.walmart.com/our-story/.
3. Joann Muller. "Runaway Toyota Recall," *Forbes*, September 29, 2009.
4. Charlie Wolf. "Digital Lifestyle: Apple Inc.," Needham & Company, February 25, 2013.
5. Stewart Thornhill and Ken Mark. *Dell Inc. in 2009,* London, ONT: Ivey Publishing, 2008.
6. Michael Kanellos and Ian Fried. "HP to Acquire Compaq for $25 billion," *CNET News*, September 4, 2001.
7. Bill Vlasic and Bradley Stertz. *Taken for a Ride: How Daimler-Benz Drove Off with Chrysler,* New York: HarperCollins, 2001.

Workshop 4

1. Michael Porter. "How Competitive Forces Shape Strategy," *Harvard Business Review* 57: 137–145.
2. "The Forbes 400: The Richest People in America." http://www.forbes.com/forbes-400/list/.
3. Bruce Einhorn. "A Former No-Name from Taiwan Builds a Global Brand," *Bloomberg Businessweek*, October 28, 2010.
4. Eric Wilson. "A Marriage of Economic Convenience," *New York Times*, November 16, 2011.
5. "U.S. Airline Mergers and Acquisitions." *Airlines for America* (A4A), http://www.airlines.org/Pages/U.S.-Airline-Mergers-and-Acquisitions.aspx
6. "Movie Theaters in the US." IBISWorld Industry Risk Rating Report 51213, May 31, 2009.
7. "Movie Theaters in the US." IBISWorld Industry Risk Rating Report 51213, June 2013.

Workshop 5

1. Michael Porter and Victor Millar. "How Information Gives You Competitive Advantage," *Harvard Business Review* 63 (1985): 149–160.

2. Mark Rogowosky. "The Death of the PC Has Not Been Exaggerated," *Forbes*, April 11, 2013.

3. Kathryn Harrigan. "Vertical Integration and Corporate Strategy," *Academy of Management Journal* 28 (1985): 397.

4. Luc Wathieu and Kevin Morris. *Apple Stores,* Boston: Harvard Business School, 2002.

5. Jad Mouawad. "Delta Buys Refinery to Get Control of Fuel Costs," *New York Times*, April 30, 2012.

6. Roger Cheng. "Sprint Gets the Nextel Monkey Off Its Back," *CNET News*, February 8, 2012.

7. Roben Farzad. "Sprint, a Distant No. 3, Limps into the Future," *Bloomberg Businessweek*, June 28, 2012.

8. Joel Bleeke and David Ernst. "Is Your Strategic Alliance Really a Sale?" *Harvard Business Review* 73 (1995): 98.

9. James Bamford. David Ernst, and David Fubini. "Launching a World-Class Joint Venture," *Harvard Business Review* 82 (2004): 90.

10. Ernst Bamford, and Fubini. "Launching a World-Class Joint Venture," 90.

11. Igor Ansoff. "Strategies for Diversification," *Harvard Business Review* 35 (1957): 118.

12. "Establishing American Honda Motor Co.." http://world.honda.com/history/challenge/1959establishingamericanhonda/index.html.

13. Chris Burritt. "Altria to Buy UST for $10.3 Billion, Gaining Skoal," *Bloomberg Businessweek*, September 8, 2008.

14. Susan Cartwright and Richard Schoenberg. "Thirty Years of Mergers and Acquisitions Research: Recent Advances and Future Opportunities," *British Journal of Management* 17 (2006): S1.

15. Keith Nunes. "Partnership Launches Crock-Pot Seasoning Mixes," *Food Business News*, April 16, 2012.

16. Andrew Martin. "Merger for SABMiller and Molson Coors," *New York Times*, October 10, 2007.

17. Jim Milliot. "Amazon Publishing Adds Over 1,000 Dorchester Titles," *Publishers Weekly*, August 31, 2012.

Workshop 6

1. Michael Porter and Victor Millar. "How Information Gives You Competitive Advantage," *Harvard Business Review* 63 (1985): 149–160.

2. Shelley DuBois. "Personality Counts: Walmart's Frugal, but Target Charms," *Fortune*, August 19, 2011.

3. "About Us." http://reedsinc.com/about-us/.

4. Reed's Inc. Form 10-K 2012. Retrieved from SEC EDGAR Web site http://www.sec.gov/edgar.shtml.

5. Reed's Inc. Form 10-K 2012.

6. Reed's Inc. Form 10-K 2012.

7. Robert Digitale. "Sonoma Sparkler Sold to LA Soda Company," *Press Democrat*, November 2, 2009.

Workshop 7

1. C. K. Prahalad and Gary Hamel. "The Core Competence of the Corporation," *Harvard Business Review* 68 (1990): 79–91.
2. ACNielsen Global Services. "What's Hot Around the Globe: Insights on Growth in Food & Beverage," Executive News Report, December 2006.
3. GE Honda Aero Engines. "Company Information," http://www.gehonda.com/company/index.html.
4. "Nike to Cease Manufacturing." *The Onion* 30, September 11, 1996.
5. McDonald's. "Getting to Know Us," http://www.aboutmcdonalds.com/mcd/our_company.html.
6. Elsa Spencer, Erica Frank, and Nicole McIntosh. "Potential Effects of the Next 100 Billion Hamburgers Sold by McDonalds," *American Journal of Preventative Medicine* 28 (2005): 379.
7. Stanley Brunn. *Wal-Mart World: The World's Biggest Corporation in the Global Economy* (New York: Routledge, 2006), 29.
8. Brooks Barnes and Michael Cieply. "Disney Swoops into Action, Buying Marvel for $4 Billion," *New York Times*, August 31, 2009.
9. Apple Inc. Form 10-K 2007, 1. Retrieved from SEC EDGAR Web site http://www.sec.gov/edgar.shtml.

Workshop 8

1. Benjamin Hoff. *The Tao of Pooh,* New York: Penguin Books, 1983: 58
2. Igor Ansoff. "Strategies for Diversification," *Harvard Business Review* 35 (957): 113–124.
3. Constantinos Markides. *All the Right Moves: A Guide to Crafting Breakthrough Strategy,* Boston: Harvard Business School Press, 2000: 83.
4. "The History of Redbox." http://www.redbox.com/history.
5. John Markoff. "Flaws Are Detected in Microsoft's Vista," *New York Times*, December 25, 2006.
6. "Crocs, Inc. Launches Latest Travel Must-Have: CitiesByFoot.com," Crocs, Inc. press release, May 15,2008, http://investors.crocs.com/phoenix.zhtml?c=193409&p=irol-IRHome, accessed June 6, 2012.
7. Michael Marks, Chuck Holloway, Hau Lee, David Hoyt, and Amanda Silverman. *Crocs: Revolutionizing an Industry's Supply Chain Model for Competitive Advantage,* Stanford, CA: Stanford Graduate School of Business, 2007.
8. "Crocs, Inc. Sells Assets of Foam Creations Business Unit," Crocs, Inc. press - release, October 6,2008, http://investors.crocs.com/phoenix.zhtml?c=193409&p=irol-IRHome, accessed October 3, 2012.

Workshop 9

1. Eric Martin. "Move Over, BRICs: Here Come the MISTs," *Bloomberg Businessweek*, August 9, 2012.
2. *The World Factbook: United States of America.* Washington, DC: Central Intelligence Agency, continually updated. https://www.cia.gov/library/publications/the-world-factbook/geos/us.html.
3. "PCs In-Use Reached over 1.6B in 2011: USA Has Nearly 311M PCs in Use." *Computer Industry Almanac Inc.*, February 2012, http://www.c-i-a.com/pr02012012.htm.
4. Michael Porter. "Competitive Advantage of Nations," *Harvard Business Review* 68 (1990): 73–93.
5. Chester Dawson. "Toyota Again World's Largest Auto Maker," *Wall Street Journal*, January 28, 2013.
6. *World Factbook: Japan.* Washington, DC: Central Intelligence Agency, continually updated. https://www.cia.gov/library/publications/the-world-factbook/geos/ja.html.
7. Michael Porter. *The Competitive Advantage of Nations* (New York: Free Press, 1990), 161.
8. Porter. *Competitive Advantage of Nations*, 167.
9. "Keiretsu: Translated Literally, It Means Headless Combine." *Economist*, October 16, 2009.
10. Federation of the Swiss Watch Industry FH. "A Short Tale of History," http://www.fhs.ch/en/history.php.
11. Tal Barak Harif. "Nasdaq Loses 'Holy Grail' Status for Offerings: Israel Overnight," *Bloomberg News*, November 7, 2011.
12. Liz Morrell. "Analysis: Evaluating Sourcing Strategies," *RetailWeek*, October 23, 2012.
13. "Tata Steel Plans Pooling of Raw Materials." *Economic Times*, June 27, 2008.
14. Indranil Bose, Shilpi Banerjee, and Edo de Vries Robbe. *Wal-mart and Bharti: Transforming Retail in India,* Hong Kong: Asia Case Research Centre—The University of Hong Kong, 2009.
15. Satish Singh and Pratyush Tripathi. "The Growth of Organized Retailing through Shopping Malls in India," *Current Trends in Technology and Science* 2 (2012): 146.
16. Nikhila Gill and Vivek Dehejia. "What Does India's Poverty Line Actually Measure?" *New York Times*, April 4, 2012.
17. Shahid Akhter and Iftekhar Equbal. "Organized Retailing in India—Challenges and Opportunities," *International Journal of Multidisciplinary Research* 2 (2012): 285.
18. A. T. Kearney. *Emerging Market Priorities for Global Retailers*, The Global Retail Development Index, n.p.: A. T. Kearney, 2006, 6.

19. *The World Factbook: India.* Washington, DC: Central Intelligence Agency, continually updated. https://www.cia.gov/library/publications/the-world-factbook/geos/in.html.

20. "Wal-Mart in India." *Wall Street Journal*, August 11, 2007.

Workshop 10

1. Scott Latham and Michael Braun. "The Performance Implications of Financial Slack During Economic Recession and Recovery: Observations from the Software Industry (2001–2003)," *Journal of Managerial Issues* 20 (2008): 30–50.

2. George Doran. "There's a S.M.A.R.T. Way to Write Management's Goals and Objectives," *Management Review* 70 (1981): 35–36.

3. "Alaska Airlines Changes Baggage Fees, Guarantees." *Pacific Business News*, June 16, 2010.

4. Sam Oches. "QSR Drive-Thru Performance Study." *QSR Special Report*, October 2011.

Workshop 11

1. Michael Porter. "What Is Strategy?" *Harvard Business Review* 74 (1996): 61–78.

2. Jim Collins. *Good to Great*, New York: HarperCollins, 2001, 13.

3. Herb Kelleher. "Customer Service: It Starts at Home," *Secured Lender* (May/June 1998): 68–73.

4. Dunkin' Donuts. "Company Snapshot," https://www.dunkindonuts.com/content/dunkindonuts/en/company.html.

Workshop 12

1. Sun Tzu. *The Art of War*, ed. and with foreword by James Clavell, New York: Delacorte Press, 1983, 28.

2. W. Chan Kim and Renee Mauborgne. *Blue Ocean Strategy: How to Create Uncontested Market Space and Make Competition Irrelevant,* Boston: Harvard Business School Press, 2005.

3. Alexander Osterwalder and Yves Pigneur. *Business Model Generation: A Handbook for Visionaries, Game Changers, and Challengers,* Hoboken, NJ: John Wiley & Sons, 2010.

4. Robert Kaplan and David Norton. *The Balanced Scorecard: Translating Strategy into Action,* Boston: Harvard Business Review Press, 1996.

Bibliography

ACNielsen Global Services. "What's Hot around the Globe: Insights on Growth in Food & Beverage." Executive News Report, December 2006.

A. T. Kearney. "*Emerging Market Priorities for Global Retailers*." The Global Retail Development Index. n.p.: A. T. Kearney, 2006.

Akhter, Shahid, and Iftekhar Equbal. "Organized Retailing in India—Challenges and Opportunities." *International Journal of Multidisciplinary Research* 2 (2012): 281–291.

Ansoff, Igor. "Strategies for Diversification." *Harvard Business Review* 35 (1957): 113–124.

Apple Inc. Form 10-K 2007, 1. Retrieved from SEC EDGAR Web site. http://www.sec.gov/edgar.shtml.

Bamford, James, David Ernst, and David Fubini. "Launching a World-Class Joint Venture." *Harvard Business Review* 82 (2004): 90–100.

Barak Harif, Tal. "Nasdaq Loses 'Holy Grail' Status for Offerings: Israel Overnight," *Bloomberg News*, November 7, 2011. http://www.businessweek.com/news/2011-11-07/nasdaq-loses-holy-grail-status-for-offerings-israel-overnight.html.

Barnes, Brooks, and Michael Cieply. "Disney Swoops into Action, Buying Marvel for $4 Billion." *New York Times*, August 31, 2009. http://www.nytimes.com/2009/09/01/business/media/01disney.html.

Berfield, Susan. "Why the McWrap Is So Important to McDonald's." *Bloomberg Businessweek*, July 3, 2013. http://www.businessweek.com/articles/2013-07-03/why-the-mcwrap-is-so-important-to-mcdonalds.

Bleeke, Joel, and David Ernst. "Is Your Strategic Alliance Really a Sale?" *Harvard Business Review* 73 (1995): 97–105.

Bose, Indranil, Shilpi Banerjee, and Edo de Vries Robbe. *Wal-mart and Bharti: Transforming Retail in India*. Hong Kong: Asia Case Research Centre—The University of Hong Kong, 2009.

Brunn, Stanley. *Wal-Mart World: The World's Biggest Corporation in the Global Economy*. New York: Routledge, 2006.

Burritt, Chris. "Altria to Buy UST for $10.3 Billion, Gaining Skoal." *Bloomberg Businessweek*, September 8, 2008. http://www.bloomberg.com/apps/news?pid =newsarchive&sid=ab6rmcKnyrK8.

Cartwright, Susan, and Richard Schoenberg. "Thirty Years of Mergers and Acquisitions Research: Recent Advances and Future Opportunities." *British Journal of Management* 17 (2006): S1–S5.

Central Intelligence Agency. "*The World Factbook: India.*" Continually updated. https://www.cia.gov/library/publications/the-world-factbook/geos/in.html.

Central Intelligence Agency. "*The World Factbook: Japan.*" Continually updated. https://www.cia.gov/library/publications/the-world-factbook/geos/ja.html.

Central Intelligence Agency. "*The World Factbook: United States of America.*" Continually updated. https://www.cia.gov/library/publications/the-world-factbook/ geos/us.html.

Cheng, Roger. "Sprint Gets the Nextel Monkey Off Its Back." *CNET News*, February 8, 2012. http://news.cnet.com/8301-1035_3-57373457-94/sprint-gets -the-nextel-monkey-off-its-back/.

Collins, James. *Good to Great: Why Some Companies Make the Leap—and Others Don't.* New York: HarperBusiness, 2001.

Computer Industry Almanac Inc. "PCs In-Use Reached Over 1.6B in 2011: USA Has Nearly 311M PCs in Use." February 2012. http://www.c-i-a.com/ pr02012012.htm.

Crocs, Inc. "Crocs, Inc. Launches Latest Travel Must-Have: CitiesByFoot.com." Crocs, Inc. press release, May 15,2008. http://investors.crocs.com/phoenix. zhtml?c=193409&p=irol-IRHome (accessed June 6, 2012).

Crocs, Inc. "Crocs, Inc. Sells Assets of Foam Creations Business Unit." Crocs, Inc. press release, October 6, 2008. http://investors.crocs.com/phoenix. zhtml?c=193409&p=irol-IRHome (accessed October 3, 2012).

Dawson, Chester. "Toyota Again World's Largest Auto Maker." *Wall Street Journal*, January 28, 2013. http://online.wsj.com/article/SB100014241278873233752 04578269181060493750.html.

Dealbook. "How the AOL-Time Warner Deal Went Wrong." *New York Times*, January 11, 2010. http://dealbook.nytimes.com/2010/01/11/how-the-aol-time -warner-deal-went-wrong/.

Digitale Robert. "Sonoma Sparkler Sold to LA Soda Company." *Press Democrat*, November 2, 2009. http://www.pressdemocrat.com/article/20091102/ BUSINESS/911029946.

Doran, George. "There's a S.M.A.R.T. Way to Write Management's Goals and Objectives." *Management Review* 70 (1981): 35–36.

DuBois, Shelley. "Personality Counts: Walmart's Frugal, but Target Charms." *Fortune*, August 19, 2011. http://management.fortune.cnn.com/2011/08/19/ personality-counts-walmart-is-frugal-but-target-charms/.

Dunkin' Donuts. "Company Snapshot." https://www.dunkindonuts.com/content/ dunkindonuts/en/company.html.

Economic Times. "Tata Steel Plans Pooling of Raw Materials." June 27, 2008. http://articles.economictimes.indiatimes.com/2008-06-27/news/27729384_1 _tata-steel-koushik-chatterjee-corus.

Economist. "Keiretsu: Translated Literally, It Means Headless Combine." October 16, 2009. http://www.economist.com/node/14299720.

Effron, Lauren. "Netflix CEO Reed Hastings Says Company Has 'Sincere Regret' Over Handling of Service Changes." *ABC News*, September 26, 2011. http://abcnews.go.com/Business/netflix-ceo-reed-hastings-company-sincere-regret -customers/story?id=14608865.

Einhron, Bruce. "A Former No-Name from Taiwan Builds a Global Brand." *Bloomberg Businessweek*, October 28, 2010. http://www.businessweek.com/magazine/content/10_45/b4202037166312.htm.

Farzad, Roben. "Sprint, a Distant No. 3, Limps into the Future." *Bloomberg Businessweek*, June 28, 2012. http://www.businessweek.com/articles/2012-06-28/sprint-a-distant-no-dot-3-limps-into-the-future.

Federation of the Swiss Watch Industry FH. "A Short Tale of History." http://www .fhs.ch/en/history.php.

"The Forbes 400: The Richest People in America." http://www.forbes.com/forbes-400/list/.

GE Honda Aero Engines. "Company Information." http://www.gehonda.com/company/index.html.

Gill, Nikhila, and Vivek Dehejia. "What Does India's Poverty Line Actually Measure?" *New York Times*, April 4, 2012. http://india.blogs.nytimes .com/2012/04/04/what-does-indias-poverty-line-actually-measure/.

Harrigan, Kathryn. "Vertical Integration and Corporate Strategy." *Academy of Management Journal* 28 (1985): 397–425.

Hoff, Benjamin. *The Tao of Pooh*. New York: Penguin Books, 1983.

Honda. "Establishing American Honda Motor Co." http://world.honda.com/history/challenge/1959establishingamericanhonda/index.html.

Isaacson, Walter. "The Real Leadership Lessons of Steve Jobs." *Harvard Business Review* 90 (2012): 92–102.

Kanellos, Michael, and Ian Fried. "HP to Acquire Compaq for $25 Billion." *CNET News*, September 4, 2001. http://news.cnet.com/2100-1001-272528.html.

Kaplan, Robert, and David Norton. *The Balanced Scorecard: Translating Strategy into Action*. Boston: Harvard Business Review Press, 1996.

Kelleher, Herb. "Customer Service: It Starts at Home." *Secured Lender* (May/June 1998): 68–73.

Kim, W. Chan, and Renee Mauborgne. *Blue Ocean Strategy: How to Create Uncontested Market Space and Make Competition Irrelevant*. Boston: Harvard Business School Press, 2005.

Latham, Scott, and Michael Braun. "The Performance Implications of Financial Slack during Economic Recession and Recovery: Observations from the Software Industry (2001-2003)." *Journal of Managerial Issues* 20 (2008): 30–50.

Markides, Constantinos. *All the Right Moves: A Guide to Crafting Breakthrough Strategy*. Boston: Harvard Business School Press, 2000.

Markoff, John. "Flaws Are Detected in Microsoft's Vista." *New York Times*, December 25, 2006. http://www.nytimes.com/2006/12/25/technology/25vista .html.

Marks, Michael, Chuck Holloway, Hau Lee, David Hoyt, and Amanda Silverman. *Crocs: Revolutionizing an Industry's Supply Chain Model for Competitive Advantage*. Stanford, CA: Stanford Graduate School of Business, 2007.

Martin, Andrew. "Merger for SABMiller and Molson Coors." *New York Times*, October 10, 2007. http://www.nytimes.com/2007/10/10/business/world business/10beer.html?_r=0.

Martin, Eric. "Move Over, BRICs. Here Come the MISTs." *Bloomberg Businessweek*, August 9, 2012. http://www.businessweek.com/articles/2012-08-09/ move-over-brics-dot-here-come-the-mists.

McDonald's. "Getting to Know Us." http://www.aboutmcdonalds.com/mcd/our_ company.html.

McGahan, Anita. "How Industries Change." *Harvard Business Review* 82 (2004): 94–104.

Milliot, Jim. "Amazon Publishing Adds Over 1,000 Dorchester Titles." *Publishers Weekly*, August 31, 2012. http://www.publishersweekly.com/pw/by-topic/ industry-news/industry-deals/article/53796-amazon-publishing-adds-over-1-000 -dorchester-titles.html.

Morrell, Liz. "Analysis: Evaluating sourcing strategies." *RetailWeek*, October 23, 2012. http://www.retail-week.com/in-business/supply-chain/analysis-evaluating -sourcing-strategies/5041994.article.

Mouawad, Jad. "Delta Buys Refinery to Get Control of Fuel Costs." *New York Times*, April 30, 2012. http://www.nytimes.com/2012/05/01/business/delta -air-lines-to-buy-refinery.html.

Mouawad, Jad. "Southwest, Determined to Expand, Buys AirTran." *New York Times*, September 27, 2010. http://www.nytimes.com/2010/09/28/business/28air .html.

"Movie Theaters in the US." IBISWorld Industry Risk Rating Report 51213. May 31, 2009.

"Movie Theaters in the US." IBISWorld Industry Risk Rating Report 51213. June 2013.

Muller, Joann. "Runaway Toyota Recall." *Forbes*, September 29, 2009. http:// www.forbes.com/2009/09/29/automobiles-toyota-recall-business-autos-toyota .html.

Neutrogena. "Why Neutrogena?" http://www.neutrogena.com/category/why+ neutrogena.do.

Nunes, Keith. "Partnership Launches Crock-Pot Seasoning Mixes." *Food Business News*, April 16, 2012. http://www.foodbusinessnews.net/News/News%20 Home/Business%20News/2012/4/Partnership%20launches%20Crock-Pot%20 seasoning%20mixes.aspx.

Oches,Sam."QSRDrive-ThruPerformanceStudy."*QSRSpecialReport*(October2011). http://www.qsrmagazine.com/reports/qsr-drive-thru-performance-study.

The Onion. "Nike to Cease Manufacturing." September 11, 1996. http://www .theonion.com/articles/nike-to-cease-manufacturing-products,1687/.

Osterwalder, Alexander, and Yves Pigneur. *Business Model Generation: A Handbook for Visionaries, Game Changers, and Challengers.* Hoboken: John Wiley & Sons, 2010.

Pacific Business News. "Alaska Airlines Changes Baggage Fees, Guarantees." June 16, 2010. http://www.bizjournals.com/pacific/stories/2010/06/14/daily22.html.

Porter, Michael. *Competitive Advantage.* New York: The Free Press, 1985.

Porter, Michael. "Competitive Advantage of Nations." *Harvard Business Review* 68 (1990): 73–93.

Porter, Michael. *The Competitive Advantage of Nations.* New York: Free Press, 1990.

Porter, Michael. "How Competitive Forces Shape Strategy." *Harvard Business Review* 57 (1979): 137–145.

Porter, Michael. "What Is Strategy?" *Harvard Business Review* 74 (1996): 61–78.

Porter, Michael, and Victor Millar. "How Information Gives You Competitive Advantage." *Harvard Business Review* 63 (1985): 149–160.

Prahalad, C. K., and Gary Hamel. "The Core Competence of the Corporation." *Harvard Business Review* 68 (1990): 79–91.

Redbox. "The History of Redbox." http://www.redbox.com/history.

Reddy, Sudeep. "Latinos Fuel Growth in Decade." *Wall Street Journal*, March 25, 2011. http://online.wsj.com/article/SB1000142405274870460470457622060 3247344790.html.

Reed's Inc. "About Us." http://reedsinc.com/about-us/.

Reed's Inc. Form 10-K 2012. Retrieved from SEC EDGAR Web site. http://www .sec.gov/edgar.shtml.

Rogowsky, Mark. "The Death of the PC Has Not Been Exaggerated." *Forbes*, April 11, 2013. http://www.forbes.com/sites/markrogowsky/2013/04/11/ the-death-of-the-pc-has-not-been-exaggerated/.

Shih, Willy, Stephen Kaufman, and David Spinola. *Netflix.* Boston: HBS Premier Case Collection, 2007.

Singh, Satish, and Pratyush Tripathi. "The Growth of Organized Retailing through Shopping Malls in India." *Current Trends in Technology and Science* 2 (2012): 146–147.

Spencer, Elsa, Erica Frank, and Nicole McIntosh. "Potential Effects of the Next 100 Billion Hamburgers Sold by McDonalds." *American Journal of Preventive Medicine* 28 (2005): 379–381.

Sun Tzu. *The Art of War.* Edited and with a foreword by James Clavell. New York: Delacorte Press, 1983.

Thornhill, Stewart, and Ken Mark. *Dell Inc. in 2009.* London, ONT: Ivey Publishing, 2008.

"U.S. Airline Mergers and Acquisitions." *Airlines for America* (A4A). http://www .airlines.org/Pages/U.S.-Airline-Mergers-and-Acquisitions.aspx.

Van Riper, Tom. "Walmart Goes Upscale." *Forbes*, August 30, 2006. http://www
.forbes.com/2006/08/30/walmart-goes-upscale-cx_tvr_0830walmart.html.

Vlasic, Bill, and Bradley Stertz. *Taken for a Ride: How Daimler-Benz Drove Off with
Chrysler*. New York: HarperCollins, 2001.

Wall Street Journal. "Wal-Mart in India." August 11, 2007. http://online.wsj.com/
article/SB118678729222894667.html.

Walmart. "Our Story." http://corporate.walmart.com/our-story/.

Walt, Vivienne. "Norway to Wal-Mart: We Don't Want Your Shares." *Fortune
Magazine*, July 24, 2006. http://money.cnn.com/magazines/fortune/fortune_
archive/2006/08/07/8382565/index.htm

Wathieu, Luc, and Kevin Morris. *Apple Stores*. Boston: Harvard Business School,
2002.

Webster's New American Dictionary. New York: Smithmark Publishers, 1995.

Weiss, Elliott, and Anwar Harahsheh. *Southwest Airlines: Keeping That Lovin' Feeling after Herb Kelleher*. Charlottesville, VA: Darden Business Publishing, 2002.

Western Union. "Our Rich History." http://corporate.westernunion.com/History
.html.

Wilson, Eric. "A Marriage of Economic Convenience." *New York Times*, November 16, 2011. http://www.nytimes.com/2011/11/17/fashion/designer-retailer
-union-remains-lucrative.html?pagewanted=all.

Wolf, Charlie. "Digital Lifestyle: Apple Inc." Needham & Company. February 25,
2013. http://clients.needhamco.com/Research/Documents/CPY203815.pdf.

Index

Note: Page numbers in *italics* indicate figures.

About the Authors

Michael R. Braun, PhD, is associate professor of management and the Poe Family Faculty Fellow at the University of Montana. Previously Michael was a director with a merchant bank, where he developed investment strategies for leading private equity firms and managed acquisitions and divestitures for private and publicly traded corporations. His early career was spent in business development in publishing, direct marketing, and e-commerce in Los Angeles, New York, and Europe, working with clients such as Staples, Autobytel, and Condé Nast Publishing. Michael lives in Missoula with his wife, Daphne, and their four children.

Scott F. Latham, PhD, currently teaches strategy at UMass Lowell, where he won the college's Teaching Excellence award in 2013. Scott worked for a dozen years in the software industry, primarily in start-up organizations, in a business development and marketing capacity. After leaving industry in 2005, he earned a PhD in strategic management. His research focuses on organizational decline, environmental turbulence, and innovation; it has been published in top journals such as *Academy of Management Review*, *Journal of Management*, *Journal of Small Business Management*, and *Journal of Business Strategy*. He has also been cited in media outlets, such as FOX, MSNBC, *Entrepreneur Magazine*, *Mass High Tech*, and the *Boston Globe*. As an executive board member at Massachusetts Medical Device Development Center (M2D2), the state's medical device incubator, he works with start-up organizations on business models, growth, and strategic positioning.